WORD PLAY:
Dictionary of Idioms

by

LILLIE POPE, Ph. D.

Illustrations by Sheila J. White, Ph. D.

Spanish Translations by Robert Mallor
Former Foreign Language Director
New York City Board of Education
Districts 21 and 22

© 1998 Lillie Pope
Brooklyn, NY
© Sheila J. White
Illustrations

Published by:
Educational Services, Inc.
BOOK LAB
PO Box 206, Ansonia Station
New York, NY 10023-0206
Telephone 212 874-5534 . 800 654.0481
Telefax 212 874-3105
Email BOOKLABpub@AOL.com

Book number: 2511
ISBN: 87594-375-6

Text and cover design: Maurice Leon
Illustrations: Sheila J. White, Ph. D.
Consultant: Robert Mallor

Printed in the United States of America

ABOUT THE AUTHOR

As Founding Director of the internationally acclaimed Language and Reading Disabilities Program at Coney Island Hospital in Brooklyn, New York, Dr. Lillie Pope's work has focused on prevention and remediation of learning problems. She has worked closely with schools, guiding teachers, paraprofessionals, volunteers and parents in how to help their students develop their language skills, with a special focus on those for whom English is a second language.

Dr. Pope, Diplomate in School Psychology, has served as Adjunct Professor at Brooklyn College and New York University, where she specialized in teacher training for the learning and language disabled, including the foreign born.

She has written the classic GUIDELINES TO TEACHING REMEDIAL READING, in addition to GUIDELINES TO TEACHING STUDENTS WITH LEARNING PROBLEMS, and co-authored SPECIAL NEEDS, SPECIAL ANSWERS. She is presently preparing GUIDELINES TO TEACHING READING

ACKNOWLEDGMENTS

I am grateful to Peter Brooks, Cecily Brown, Kirby Han, Felicia Hyatt, Rosemary LaRosa, Milton Mino, Deborah Pope, Miriam Pope, Esther Tucker and Marie White for their generous investment of time and suggestions. This book would not have been possible without the gracious and patient assistance of my husband, Martin Pope.

I am indebted to Robert Mallor, linguist and educational consultant, who provided not only a rigorous translation of the English definitions into Spanish, but also shared his expertise in the English language. I am further indebted to Martha Alavo for her kind patience and attention during stressful times.

I must convey my appreciation of and gratitude to Dr. Sheila White for her many suggestions, as well as her artistic renderings of the literal translations of some of the idioms. Her experience in linguistics, in research with animals and the hearing impaired, the learning disabled, and English as a second language combined to enrich the art that she created for this book.

I ask forgiveness of all who assisted whom I have failed to mention.

INTRODUCTION

Learning a language begins with the building of a vocabulary. This vocabulary consists mainly of words and expressions whose meaning can be understood from the definition of each word: **The table is brown; we eat lunch at noon; she is a pretty girl**. Those who are learning the English language, and have mastered standard English, are repeatedly frustrated by expressions that do not make sense when each word is interpreted literally. Idioms (and slang) are examples of such language.

Idioms are words or expressions in a given language that are peculiar to that language, and cannot be understood by defining each word individually. They are expressions that may be metaphors, or slang, or allusions to objects or events that a native-born person would usually recognize. Idiomatic expressions give language its color and vitality. They are forceful, emotional, and sometimes humorous formulations that are used in place of standard expressions. They are indispensable and they enrich the spoken and written language. They make simple ideas more dramatic, more vivid, more colorful: **"He shed crocodile tears"** is more concise and more dramatic than **"He is a hypocrite; he is pretending to be sad, but he doesn't really mean it."** Those of us who have spoken English all of our lives are not conscious of the rather large number of such expressions that we use as we speak and write informally.

Although idioms add color to language, they present difficulties for people with language problems, those for whom English is a second language, and for children. If these individuals were to interpret at face value statements like **"My eyes popped when I heard that story," "I work around the clock,"** or **"You're pulling my leg,"** they would be confused and embarrassed because they would not understand the message. An amusing translation by a foreign-born speaker clearly demonstrates the problem. Presented with the statement,

"The spirit is willing, but the flesh is weak," the interpretation was **"The liquor is OK, but the meat is bad."**

Slang, which may be considered a sub-group of idioms, consists of expressions that are known to people in a particular group or sub-culture: **"Man, you're hip"** (or **"hep to the jive"**) for example, means **"You certainly understand what is going on."** Slang is used to bind those within the group, and sometimes to exclude others; it is occasionally used to shock the listener.

Interestingly, slang terms often are "down-putting", and are used for name-calling. They express fear and distrust of persons from whom we want to distance ourselves. Rather than saying **"This person is inferior in some way,"** he may be called a **wimp, a nerd, a banana brain, boob, chump, dimwit, dolt, dope, dunce, jerk, klutz, knothead, knucklehead, lame brain, lowbrow, nincompoop, nitwit, sap** or a score of other names. It is interesting to understand that each of these words reflects a slightly different meaning to "being stupid." Choosing the correct term in slang is often as delicate and precise a decision as using the correct word in standard English.

Our language changes rapidly; new words emerge with each new advance, while some old words take on new meanings. For example, a **virus** is now deadly for the computer, in addition to being a carrier of disease. Some new vocabulary has already found its way into the standard dictionary, while a growing pool of new expressions remains in the general spoken vocabulary, waiting to see if growing usage over time warrants its entry into the standard dictionary.

This dictionary presents more than 1,200 of the most frequently used idioms (and slang expressions) in the English language; most of them are not now defined in the standard dictionary. Each idiom is defined in English, as well as in Spanish (the most common native language of United States immigrants), followed by one or more examples of its usage in English. Space is provided for translation into the native language of the student, if it is other than Spanish, and for the student to write his/her own example of its usage.

It has been frustrating to limit the number of idioms defined here; the selection has been based on careful listening, on attention to current speech in the media and in everyday life, on consultation with teachers and persons for whom English is a second language, and finally on my own judgment. Each term is followed by a definition and an example of how that term is used; these will help the reader grasp the meaning of each term. I have tried to keep my language simple and to avoid using idioms as part of the definition of a term.

GENERAL CHARACTERISTICS OF IDIOMS

• Each idiom has a precise form; if the words are rearranged, it loses its meaning: **"She broke her neck to get the job done"** cannot be rearranged to **"Her neck was broken to get the job done."** **"Winning the medal was a feather in her cap"** is not the same as **"Her cap had a feather in it for winning the medal."**

• Although most idioms become meaningless when their words are rearranged, some two-word idioms, however, can be separated; in this dictionary, most of the variations are listed exactly as they may be used. For example, **"ease someone out"** may also be expressed as **"ease out someone."** **"Trade in something"** may also be expressed as **"trade something in."**

• Many idioms lean on words related to body parts: **lend an ear, an eye for an eye, you're pulling my leg, he's pulled the wool over your eyes, all thumbs.**

• Food and food-related words are very common. Often the food means money, as in **cabbage, lettuce, bread.** Sometimes food words relate to people: **nuts, fruitcake, cold fish, honey, sugar, sweetie pie.**

• With the passage of time, some idioms fade into oblivion, to be replaced by others. For example **23, skidoo**, popular half a century ago, and meaning **"Get away from me"** is seldom heard today, as is **the cat's meow**, meaning "the greatest".

• Idioms differ from language to language; it is interesting to find that many English idioms have similar versions in other languages.

HOW TO USE THIS BOOK

• To find a word or expression in this book, look for one of the key words. These are listed alphabetically. As an example, for **spill the beans**, look under **spill** or **beans**. Under **beans**, it is defined, and an example of its usage is given. Under the key word **spill**, the expression is listed with a * next to the word **beans**. This tells you to look for the definition under the key word **beans**.

• Note also that the same word, used in different idioms, may have a completely different meaning in each case: for example, **blow** a fuse, **blow** the whistle, have a **blow**-out, **blow** off steam, etc.

• Not included as key words are frequently used pronouns, conjunctions, prepositions and words that do not add significantly to the meaning of the phrase. A list of the words omitted is on this page.

• Omitted as key words are those that do not add significantly to the meaning of the idiom:

    1) Letters of the alphabet are not used as key words, except A, P, Q, T.

    2) Some directional words are not key words in this book, such as **above, across**. The following directional words are listed as
key words: **about, around, off, out, up, down, beside, on, over, through, under**.

    3) Prepositions, conjunctions and connectives, such as **if, but, and** are omitted. Included in this dictionary's key words are **even, just, till, together**.

    4) Pronouns, such as **I, me, we** are omitted. Included are **who, you**.

    5) Passive verbs, such as **am, be, been, have been, is, was** are not key words.

    6) **Someone, something, anyone, anything, one's, oneself** are not listed as key words.

• When the definition of an idiom begins with the word **to** or **be**, the idiom may be considered to be a verb and conjugated like a verb. For example,

the definition of **get held up** starts with the word **to**. The idiom may therefore be used in the past, future and other tenses, when appropriate. "Joe **got** held up. Joe **will get** held up if he delays much longer. Mary **would have gotten** held up if she had waited for Joe."

• Some idioms (usually exclamatory) are used only in the present tense, and may never be conjugated or varied in any way. You will find this noted next to each idiom that allows no variation at all. For example, **Drop dead!, Get off it!, Get lost!** or **Hold your horses!** must always be in the present tense, and cannot be varied at all.

• It is important to distinguish between **one** and **someone** in idiomatic expressions. **One** usually refers to the subject, the person making the statement, as in **eat one out of house and home**, or **get one's feet wet**. **Someone** usually refers to someone else, as in **get on someone's nerves**.

• In parentheses ( ) you will find an alternate word or words that may sometimes be used in the same expression, and with the same meaning, as **beef (bellyache, complain)**.

• Next to each idiom is its meaning in Spanish, together with a blank space in which it is suggested that you write its meaning in your native language. Here you may also write a sentence in English that uses that idiom. This will help you learn the meanings of these terms more rapidly. Following is an example of what you may do:

burst out laughing
to start laughing
Jody made such a funny face that
I burst out laughing.

French student: *éclater de rire*

German student: *in gelächter ausbrechen*

vii

• Remember that this dictionary will help you to understand the idioms that you hear and read. After you understand an expression very well, and have heard it and understood it many times, you may then use it in informal conversation, preferably in the classroom.

• Use this dictionary to find the meaning and usage of the idioms in question; use the standard dictionary for other definitions. Get into the Dictionary Habit!

HOW TO TEACH

• All of your students must learn to understand the difference between a literal and a figurative statement. Discuss the meaning of this statement: **"To finish building this table on time, I worked around the clock."** Does this mean that I put a clock in the center of the room, and built the table around it? **"He drives me up a wall."** What does that mean? Does he get into an automobile, and drive me to a wall, and then he drives the car up the wall? Is that possible? Is that what it means?

• Because our primary goal is to teach students the meaning of figurative language, each idiom is followed by its meaning (definition) both in English and in Spanish. The corresponding Spanish idiom is omitted. Those who tend to interpret language literally will have difficulty in understanding the meanings of idioms/figurative words and phrases in any language, unless they are carefully guided; those who are more advanced will need less guidance.

• Have the students find examples of figurative language — of language that should not be interpreted literally — in books, on TV, and in the conversation that they hear. Let them bring in those words and expressions. Look up their meanings. For those that are not in this dictionary, have each student create his own supplementary Word Book; let the students discuss these words, listen carefully, and use them in class. Let them enter the words, definitions, and usage in their own books. If they

are so inclined, let them draw pictures to illustrate the incorrect or literal meanings. This will give them pleasure, and help them remember the correct meanings.

• Work slowly and patiently. Emphasize spoken language until the students are facile with the words and expressions. The only written work at the outset should be in making the entries into their own Word Books, and on the lines set out below each idiom. As they become comfortable with expressions, they should be encouraged to use them in their writings (compositions, letters, stories, etc.).

• If your students speak and read Spanish, the Spanish definitions in the dictionary will be helpful to them. If their first language is other than Spanish, discuss the words and phrases as they come up in spoken and written language in the classroom, and help them translate the meanings into their primary languages. Have students explore whether English idioms are matched by similar idioms in their native language. Have them make lists of idioms in their primary languages that enrich their language, and help give them a greater appreciation of and respect for English idioms.

• Have your students categorize the idioms: which idioms deal with body parts--the arms, the legs, eyes, ears, etc.? Which deal with food? How many are complimentary? Which ones are derogatory? Which are sexist? Which ones are always negative? Which ones deal with sex, romance, love? Which deal with frustration? The grouping and analysis of idiomatic language is fascinating. Students will be interested and will expand their vocabularies.

• Learning to understand and use the subtleties of idiomatic expressions in English takes time and patience. With your support and encouragement, your students will be quite successful. Perhaps it will interest them to know the top 10 words used by Shakespeare (in TOP TEN OF EVERYTHING, Ed. (US) Jill Hamilton, 1996) are **the, and, I, to, of, a, you, my, that, in**. Your students should be reassured that, despite their feelings of frustration, they are well on their way to learning the English language.

• Remember that our purpose here is to help the students understand idioms and to help them learn to express themselves in English in a relaxed way. We do not attempt here to teach grammar.

A

FROM A TO Z
complete; from beginning to end
[desde el comienzo hasta el fin]
Lucy has learned her mother's recipes from A to Z.

ABOUT
BE **NUTS*** ABOUT
UP* AND ABOUT

ACCOUNT
TAKE INTO ACCOUNT
to include something or someone in making a
decision or a calculation
[incluir algo para tomar una decisión
o calcular algo]
*Marion had to take into account her rent, carfare,
and cost of lunch when planning her monthly budget.*

ACT
ACT REAL (BE REAL)
to be realistic or practical; not to fantasize
[ser realista o práctico]
*Be real; you can't go out into the storm
without a coat.*

READ THE RIOT ACT
to scold threateningly
[reñir con amenazas]
*Tom's mother read the riot act to him, forbidding
him to leave the house after eight o'clock at night.*

AGAINST
GO AGAINST THE **GRAIN***
UP AGAINST THE **WALL***

AGE
TO BE OF AGE

to reach the age required by law (usually 18 for
driving, 18 for voting.)
[cumplir la edad indicada de la ley (generalmente
18 años para manejar un coche, 21 años para votar)]
Nancy can hardly wait to be of age for driving a car.

AIR
AIR ONE'S DIRTY LINEN IN PUBLIC
to talk about personal and private troubles in public
[hablar en público sobre las dificultades personales
y privadas]
*Married people discussing their personal problems
on TV are just airing their dirty linen in public.*

CLEAR THE AIR
to remove misunderstandings
[quitar los malentendimientos]
*Lily asked the group what was bothering each
one of them. The discussion cleared the air.*

HOT AIR
exaggerated or untruthful information
[información exagerada o no cierta]
*Frank's claim about his excellent school grades
was a lot of hot air.*

ALL
ALL **EARS***
ALL IN
exhausted
[agotado; rendido]
I've just finished changing two flat tires, and I'm all in.

ALL **THUMBS***
ALL **WET***

I

ALLEY

UP ONE'S ALLEY

something that lies within one's skills or interests

[algo que está dentro de las habilidades o el interes de alguien]

Lillian is a fine ice-skater and loves children. Teaching them how to ice skate is right up her alley.

ALONG

STRING* SOMEONE ALONG

AMUCK

RUN AMUCK (ALSO RUN AMOK)

to be crazed with frenzy; to do violence

[estar enloquecido de frenesí]

After smoking crack for the first time, Joe ran amuck in the street, hitting everyone he could reach.

ANTS

HAVE ANTS IN ONE'S PANTS

to be restless

[estar inquieto]

He never sits still during dinner; he acts as if he has ants in his pants.

APART

COME APART AT THE SEAMS

to fail at the weak points

[fallar en los puntos débiles]

Tina's great plan to enroll boys and girls on the soccer team came apart at the seams.

FALL APART

(1) to fail

[fracasar]

His bad marriage finally fell apart.

(2) to break into pieces

[despedazar]

He drove that car until it fell apart.

TELL (TWO THINGS OR PEOPLE) APART

to distinguish between two things or people that look very much alike

[distinguir entre dos cosas o dos personas que son muy parecidas]

Tina and Dina are identical twins. I can't tell them apart.

APPLE

APPLE OF ONE'S EYE

favorite; someone in whom one takes great pride

[favorita persona]

Bobby is the apple of his mother's eye.

APPLE-PIE ORDER

in perfect order

[perfectamente ordenado]

Tom is very neat. His desk is in apple-pie order.

APPLE-POLISHER

one who seeks favor by flattery

[alguien que busca la aprobación halagando al prójimo]

Our teacher, Mrs. Boym, discourages apple-polishers.

UPSET THE APPLE-**CART***

ARM

(COST) AN ARM AND A LEG

excessive cost; usually a lot of money

[un ojo de la cara]

He charged me an arm and a leg to repair my automobile.

TWIST SOMEONE'S ARM
to force someone (usually with words) to do some thing

[obligarle a alguien hacer algo (usualmente por medio de las palabras)]

Nellie's mother twisted Nellie's arm to get her to mop the floor.

ARMS
BE UP IN ARMS
to be ready to fight

[estar preparado a luchar]

Howard was up in arms when he heard that the landlord planned to raise the rent 20%.

AROUND
BEAT* AROUND THE BUSH
BUM* AROUND
FIDDLE* AROUND
KID* AROUND
KNOCK* (KICK) SOMETHING AROUND
LEAD* ONE AROUND BY THE NOSE
MONKEY* AROUND WITH
PUSH* SOMEONE AROUND
RUN AROUND IN CIRCLES*
SHOP* AROUND
STICK* AROUND
TURN* AROUND
WORK AROUND THE CLOCK*

ATTACHED
STRINGS ATTACHED
additional requirements

[requisitos adicionales]

Mary was surprised that there were strings attached to her child care job: she had to take care of other children that came to visit.

ATTITUDE
ATTITUDE
sullen, hostile, uncooperative, negative, resistant, suspicious manner

[aire hosco, hóstil, no cooperativo, negativo, resistente, sospechoso]

Mary comes to class with an attitude. She never smiles, she is sullen and suspicious, and never works with the class.

AWAY
BE (GET) CARRIED* AWAY

AXE
AN AXE TO GRIND
a grievance

[queja]

He had an axe to grind at that meeting; he voted against the motions because he was angry that he had not been appointed president.

GET THE AXE
to be fired from a position

[ser despedido del empleo]

If John did not get the axe during this round of firings, he will in the next.

BACK
BACK OUT OF
to withdraw from a commitment

[retirarse de]

Joe backed out of his promise to help us move the furniture.

BACK SEAT DRIVER
one who directs activities, but is not directly responsible

[alguien que dirige las actividades, pero que no es directamente responsable]

Mary is a back seat driver: she always tells Jane what to do even though she has no right to do so.

BE BACK ON ONE'S FEET
to return to a normal (previous) status

[regresar a un estado normal (anterior)]

Six weeks after her surgery, Lois was back on her feet, working a full schedule.

3

BACK TO THE DRAWING BOARD
to prepare a revised plan; to start all over again
[preparar un plan revisado]
The school board did not like the plan for the new high school; it was back to the drawing board for the architect.

BEHIND SOMEONE'S BACK
without one's knowledge
[sin que alguien lo sepa]
Joseph found a new job for himself. He did it behind his employer's back.

GET OFF SOMEONE'S BACK
to stop annoying someone; leave someone alone
[dejar de molestar a alguien]
Andrew felt that he was being supervised too closely. He did better work when the boss got off his back.

HAVE ONE'S BACK TO THE WALL
to be desperate
[estar desesperado]
Jack could not pay back the money he owed the bank. He had his back to the wall because he had just lost his job.

SET* SOMEONE BACK
STAB* SOMEONE IN THE BACK
TALK BACK TO SOMEONE
to challenge openly
[retar abiertamente]
When the teacher scolded Maria for making noise in class, Maria talked back to the teacher, telling her to mind her own business.

BACKWARD

BEND OVER BACKWARD
(1) to give someone more than a fair share
[proporciónar a alquien más que lo justo]

Neal bent over backward and gave his brother more than half of the marbles to be sure to be fair.

---

(2) to require more than is usual so that one may not be accused of being lenient
[exigirle a uno más que lo normal para no ser acusado de ser benevolo]
Two sons of our scoutmaster are in our troop. He is stricter with them than with the other boys; he bends over backward, to be sure of being fair to the other boys.

BACON

BRING HOME THE BACON
to earn money that supports the household
[ganar el dinero que sostiene a la familia]
Paul is the only one working; he brings home the bacon every Friday.

BAD

BAD BLOOD
bad feeling between people
[malos sentimientos entre las personas]
Marisa has not spoken to her aunt in thirty years. There has been bad blood between them because of an old quarrel.

BAD EGG
a bad person
[persona mala]
One person in that gang is a bad egg. He will end up in prison.

BAD-MOUTH SOMEONE OR SOMETHING
to speak badly about (criticize) someone or something
[denunciar (criticar) a alquien (algo)]
The paint dealer bad-mouthed his competitor to each of his customers.

BAG

BAG AND BAGGAGE
with all of one's possessions
[con todas las posesiones de alguien]
When Henry was 21, he moved out of his parents' home, bag and baggage.

BE LEFT HOLDING THE BAG
to be left with the blame or the responsibility for something
[quedarse con la culpa o la responsabilidad por algo]
Three of the five who ate lunch left before paying their shares. Susan was left holding the bag. She paid the bill.

BROWN BAG
to bring lunch from home (usually in a brown bag), to work
[llevar el almuerzo de casa (generalmente en una bolsa de color café) al trabajo]
When I want to save money, I brown bag my lunch, and take it to work.

IN THE BAG
definite; guaranteed to happen
[definitivo]
When the salesman visited Eastern Mills, the buyer liked his merchandise. The saleman thought that the order was in the bag.

LET THE CAT OUT OF THE BAG
to reveal a secret
[revelar un secreto]
Joan promised not to tell anyone about Ira's engagement, but she did. She let the cat out of the bag.

BAGGAGE
BAG* AND BAGGAGE

BAIL

BAIL SOMEONE OUT
to rescue someone from a difficult situation
[rescatar a alguien de una situación defícil]
When Maria forgot to arrange for transportation for the class, Ken bailed her out by getting the bus passes.

BAKED

HALF-BAKED
incomplete; not well thought out
[mal pensado]
The class was eager to take the trip to Washington; they were disappointed when they heard Amos' half-baked plan to get the money by selling pickles.

BAKER'S

BAKER'S DOZEN
thirteen: one dozen plus one
[trece]
Doughnuts were on sale for two dollars for a baker's dozen.

BALL

BEHIND* THE EIGHT-BALL
CARRY THE BALL
to take the responsibility for a program or project
[aceptar la responsabilidad por un programa o un proyecto]
John and David both went their employer to ask for an increase in salary, but David carried the ball by doing all the talking.

HAVE A BALL
to have a wonderful time
[divertirse mucho]
I had a ball looking through the books in those cartons.

5

HAVE A LOT ON THE BALL
to be bright, to be smart
[ser listo]
> Danny is a very capable youngster. He has a lot on the ball.

KEEP THE BALL ROLLING
to avoid interruption for something that is going on
[evitar interrupciones en algo que está en marcha]
> John signed the petition to save the park. He kept the ball rolling.

ON THE BALL
in control of a situation
[controlando una situación]
> Adam forgot that his income tax was due on Friday, but his wife was on the ball and mailed it in on time.

START THE BALL ROLLING
to start something going
[poner algo en marcha]
> Kenneth urged Rena to begin baking for the holiday party. He started the ball rolling by baking the first cake.

THROW SOMEONE A **CURVE*** BALL

BALLPARK

BALLPARK FIGURE
an estimated amount, not exact
[una cantidad aproximada, no exacta]
> Mr. Steens asked the contractor for a ballpark figure for the cost of building the porch.

BALONEY

IT'S A LOT OF BALONEY.
It is nonsense, fantasy, untrue
[Es un disparate.]
> Joe's story about winning all that money is a lot of baloney.

BANANAS

GO BANANAS
to become crazy, insane
[volverse uno loco]
> I almost went bananas when I found out how much work still had to be done.

BAND

BEAT* THE BAND

BANDIT

MAKE OUT LIKE A BANDIT
to make a lot of profit; to gain a lot
[sacar mucho beneficio]
> When Charles opened his computer shop, he was very successful. He made out like a bandit.

BANDWAGON

GET (JUMP, CLIMB) ON THE BANDWAGON
to join, or agree with, or go along with a popular group
[unirse, o ponerse uno de acuerdo con un movimiento popular]
> Mary was told that all her friends bought hats for the party; she got on the bandwagon and got one too.

BANG

GET A KICK (BANG, CHARGE) OUT OF SOMEONE OR SOMETHING
to enjoy, to get pleasure from someone or something
[gozar de]
> I love to listen to New Orleans jazz. I get a bang (kick, charge) out of it.

_____

BARK

ONE'S BARK IS WORSE THAN ONE'S BITE

One appears to be more angry (ferocious, aggressive) than one actually is.

[uno parece estar más enojado (feroz o agresivo) de lo que está en realidad]

My mother says she will throw out my TV set, because I haven't cleaned my room, but her bark is worse than her bite.

_____

BARK UP THE WRONG TREE

to take an incorrect approach (solution) to a problem

[tratar de resolver un problema de una manera no apropiada]

When John insulted the prize-fighter, he was barking up the wrong tree.

_____

BARREL

LOCK, STOCK AND BARREL

including everything; completely

[con todo incluido]

Mr. Robins bought the store, its merchandise, and its debts. He took it over lock, stock and barrel.

_____

OVER A BARREL

in a difficult spot, and with no choice left

[en una situación difícil y sin alternativa]

Saul had to sell his car to pay the rent. He was over a barrel.

_____

SCRAPE THE BOTTOM OF THE BARREL

to take what is left

[aceptar lo que haya]

The company had to hire people with no experience for the job. They had to scrape the bottom of the barrel.

_____

BASE

GET TO FIRST BASE

to make a little progress, make a start

[hacer un poco de progreso, dar los primeros pasos]

Jane has an appointment for an interview for a job. At least she got to first base.

_____

BAT

BAT A THOUSAND

to do something exceptionally well

[hacer also excepcionalmente bien]

WEST SIDE STORY was very well-received on Broadway. Bernstein definitely batted a thousand when he wrote that show.

_____

GO TO BAT FOR

to defend

[defender]

When he was arrested, Bill's brother needed a lawyer to go to bat for him.

_____

NOT TO BAT AN EYELASH

to give the appearance of not being surprised

[parecer uno no estar sorprendido]

Henry does not get excited easily. He did not bat an eyelash when he learned that he had won one thousand dollars in the lottery.

_____

RIGHT OFF THE BAT

immediately; right away

[inmediatamente]

When I interviewed Mrs. Temple for a job, she told me what salary she expected right off the bat.

_____

BAY

HOLD SOMEONE OR SOMETHING AT BAY

to keep someone or something from escaping or advancing

7

[evitar que alguien o algo se escape o avance]
The lone policeman held the entire group of thieves at bay with his hand gun.

_____

BE

BE OUT OF SOMETHING
to have no more supplies of something
[agotarse de los abastecimientos]
Because of the recent snowstorms, the corner grocery is out of all dairy products.

_____

BE UP TO SOMETHING
(1) to be capable of (doing something)
[ser capaz de (hacer algo)]
Since Grandpa is 75 years old, I don't think he is up to clearing the snow from the blizzard.

_____

(2) to be planning something not known to others
[planear algo desconocido a los demas]
Tim has been acting very peculiarly lately. I wonder what he is up to.

_____

BEANS

SPILL THE BEANS
to tell (reveal) a secret
[divulgar un secreto]
Murray was asked not to tell anyone about his pay raise, but he was so excited that he spilled the beans to all his friends.

_____

BEAR

BEAR IN MIND SOMETHING; BEAR SOMETHING IN MIND
to remember
[tener en cuenta]
When you make your budget, bear in mind that you will have to pay the installment for your car on the first of each month.

_____

BEAT

BEAT AROUND THE BUSH
to avoid answering a question or coming to the point
[evitar el responder a una pregunta o el llegar al caso]
When the teacher asked Simon why he did not do his homework, he beat around the bush, talking instead about the car accident near the school.

_____

BEAT SOMEONE TO THE PUNCH (DRAW)
to do something before someone else, who also planned to do it
[hacer algo antes de otra persona, que también pensaba hacerlo]
Leonard knew that Joanne was planning to announce his promotion as supervisor. He beat her to the punch by announcing it first.

_____

BEAT THE PANTS OFF SOMEONE
to be the clear winner in a quarrel, dispute or fight
[salir ganador obvio en una riña, disputa o lucha]
Sam beat the pants off Victor in a game of handball.

_____

BEAT THE RAP
to avoid the punishment, usually for a crime
[evitar el castigo, usualmente por un crimen]
The thief knew he was going to be arrested, but he beat the rap by fleeing to South America.

_____

TO BEAT THE BAND
with a lot of energy
[con mucha energiá]
The children hammered away to beat the band.

_____

BEATING

TAKE A BEATING
to lose position, or an argument, or money
[perder prestigio, una disputa, o dinero]

When the stock market crashed, Mr. Major took a beating. He lost all his money.

BEAVER
EAGER BEAVER
hardworking person, eager to please
[persona aplicada, dedicada a complacer a los demás]
Melvin is an eager beaver. He always does more than is called for.

BECK
AT SOMEONE'S BECK AND CALL
ready to obey or assist someone, at a moment's notice
[preparado a obedecer o ayudar a otra persona, a cualquier hora]
Arnold's secretary was at his beck and call.

BED
GET UP ON THE WRONG SIDE OF THE BED
to be in a bad mood
[estar de mal humor]
Tom is very irritable today. He acts like he got up on the wrong side of the bed.

NO BED OF ROSES
not a good situation; a difficult situation
[una situación mala o difícil]
Gretchen took a summer job as waitress in a cheap restaurant; it was no bed of roses.

BEE
BEE IN ONE'S BONNET
a fixed thought or idea that remains in one's head; an obsession
[un pensamiento fijo o una idea que se queda en la mente de alguien; una obsesión]
Mrs. Lane has a bee in her bonnet: she insists that her neighbors make a block party.

BEEF
BELLYACHE (ALSO BEEF, GRIPE, KICK, SQUAWK)
to complain
[quejarse]
Susan never stops beefing about her employer, who makes her work overtime.

BEFORE
BEFORE YOU **CAN*** SAY JACK ROBINSON
COUNT ONE'S **CHICKENS*** BEFORE THEY ARE HATCHED
PUT THE **CART*** BEFORE THE HORSE

BEHIND
BEHIND ONE'S **BACK***
BEHIND THE EIGHT-BALL
in a difficult position
[en una situación difícil]
I lost my week's wages at the race track. Now I'm behind the eight-ball with my wife.

WET BEHIND THE EARS
without experience; naive
[sin experiencia]
Steven is a beginning teacher, and does not know how to manage the class; he is wet behind the ears.

BEING
FOR THE TIME BEING
for now; temporarily
[por ahora]
This snack will be enough for the time being. We will have a proper meal when we get home.

BELIEVE
MAKE BELIEVE
to pretend
[fingir]

*Look under the **key word*** for this idiom.

Make believe that you are a queen. How would you treat your subjects?

```
[                                    ]
[_____]
```

MAKE-BELIEVE
> fantasies
> [fantasia]
> > *The stories Mel tells you about his wealth are all make-believe.*

```
[                                    ]
[_____]
```

BELL
RING A BELL
> to serve as a reminder
> [servir como recuerdo]
> > *Whenever I pass the Hippodrome Parking Lot, it rings a bell; it reminds me of the Hippodrome Theatre where I saw my first opera.*

```
[                                    ]
[_____]
```

BELLYACHE
BELLYACHE
> see BEEF*

BELOW
HIT BELOW THE **BELT***

BELT
HIT BELOW THE BELT; HIT SOMEONE BELOW THE BELT
> to be unfair to someone
> [ser injusto con alguien]
> > *Susan taunted her friend for being too heavy. That was hitting below the belt.*

```
[                                    ]
[_____]
```

TIGHTEN ONE'S BELT
> to economize; spend less money
> [economizar]
> > *John lost his job. He knew that he would have to tighten his belt in order to survive without his salary.*

```
[                                    ]
[_____]
```

BEND
BEND OVER **BACKWARD***

BEND SOMEONE'S **EAR***

BENDER
FENDER*-BENDER

BENEFIT
FRINGE BENEFITS
> benefits to which an employee is entitled on a particular job, usually holidays, vacation, sick pay, health insurance, and perhaps more
> [beneficios que tiene un empleado en su trabajo, usualmente los días feriados, las vacaciones, el salario durante una ausencia por enfermedad, el seguro de la salud, y posiblemente más]
> > *Julia took the job because it had excellent fringe benefits, such as health insurance and sick pay.*

```
[                                    ]
[_____]
```

BESIDE
BE BESIDE ONESELF
> to be very angry
> [estar enfurecido]
> > *When Mr. Cruikshank saw the damage the vandals had done to his automobile, he was beside himself with anger.*

```
[                                    ]
[_____]
```

BESIDE THE **POINT***

BEST
GIVE IT ONE'S BEST SHOT
> to do the best one can do
> [hacer lo mejor que se puede]
> > *Joanne really wanted to win the marathon. She gave it her best shot.*

```
[                                    ]
[_____]
```

BETTER
GET THE BETTER OF SOMEONE
> to win out over someone
> [salir uno el ganador]
> > *He got the better of me in that chess game.*

```
[                                    ]
[_____]
```

BIDE
BIDE ONE'S TIME
> to wait until a better moment (time)
> [esperar hasta un momento más oportuno]

I want to buy an automobile, but I am biding my time until the prices go down.

[blank box]

BIG

BIG DEAL
an important event
[un suceso de importancia]]
Jorge thought getting an A in Math was no big deal.

[blank box]

BIG SHOT
an important person
[alguien importante]
*John is a big shot at the Yankee Stadium.
He got me a free ticket to the game.*

[blank box]

GIVE SOMEONE A BIG HAND; GIVE A BIG HAND TO SOMEONE
to applaud someone enthusiastically
[aplaudir mucho a alguien]
*After his speech, they gave the speaker
a big hand.*

[blank box]

BILL

CLEAN BILL OF HEALTH
healthy diagnosis, with no problems
[una díagnosis de buena salud, sin problemas]
*Bill was pleased that the doctor, after examining
him, gave him a clean bill of health.*

[blank box]

FILL THE BILL
to meet all the requirements
[cumplir con todos los requisitos]
*This vase is exactly what I need for the flowers.
It fills the bill.*

[blank box]

FOOT THE BILL
to pay

[pagar la cuenta]
*When savings and loan associations failed, the
government had to foot the bill.*

[blank box]

PAD THE BILL
to increase a fee or account dishonestly, by including inappropriate items or amounts
[aumentar una cuenta deshonradamente,
incluyendo artículos o cantidades incorrectos]
*I always inspect the restaurant bill carefully,
because some places pad the bill.*

[blank box]

SELL SOMEONE A BILL OF GOODS; SELL A BILL OF GOODS TO SOMEONE
to persuade someone by exaggerating or deceiving
[persuadir a alguien exagerando o engañando]
*Don't believe what that salesman says. He's
selling you a bill of goods.*

[blank box]

BIN
LOONY*-BIN

BIND

IN A BIND
in a difficult situation
[en circunstancias difíciles]
*When I'm in a bind for cash, I know I can ask my
Aunt Reva for a loan.*

[blank box]

BIRDS

BIRDS OF A FEATHER
persons who are similar in some way
[personas que son parecidas en algún aspecto]
*The skiers on the ski slopes are athletic, muscular
and courageous — they are birds of a feather.*

[blank box]

FOR THE BIRDS
worthless
[sin valor]

That movie is too long, and it is boring. It is for the birds.

KILL TWO BIRDS WITH ONE STONE

to solve two problems at the same time

[resolver dos problemas a la misma vez]

Katrina went across town to the store so that she could kill two brids with one stone by buying groceries and visiting her boy friend who worked there.

BIRTHDAY

IN ONE'S BIRTHDAY SUIT

naked; wearing no clothes

[desnudo]

At the nudist beach, people swim in their birthday suits.

BITE

BITE OFF MORE THAN ONE CAN CHEW

to try to do too much

[tratar de hacer demasiado]

Ned could not finish building the porch alone. He had bitten off more than he could chew.

BITE SOMEONE'S HEAD OFF

to scold; show one's anger to someone

[reñir a alguien]

Melissa's father almost bit her head off for coming home so late.

BITE ONE'S TONGUE

to regret having said something; refrain from saying something

[sentir haber dicho algo; dejar de decir algo]

I bit my tongue after asking Mrs. Perkins how old she is.

BITE THE **BULLET***

BITE THE HAND THAT FEEDS YOU

to hurt the person who helps you

[danar a la persona que le ayuda a uno]

Tony bit the hand that fed him when he refused to help his father unload the car.

HIS **BARK*** IS WORSE THAN HIS BITE

PUT* THE BITE ON SOMEONE

BLACK

BLACK SHEEP

of several children in a family, the one who disgraces the family

[de los hijos de una familia, el que la humilla]

Ivan was the black sheep in the Stewart family; he was often in jail.

POT **CALLING*** THE KETTLE BLACK (THE)

BLANKET

WET BLANKET

one who destroys the pleasure in an event

[aguafiestas]

Mary was a wet blanket at my birthday party. She criticized all my gifts.

BLAST

HAVE A BLAST

to have a wonderful time

[divertirse mucho]

We had a blast at our anniversary party. The food and music were great.

BLIND

BLIND DATE

an appointment or date arranged for two people who do not know each other

[una cita arreglada entre dos personas que no se conocen]

Sheila wore her new dress for her blind date last Saturday.

BLINK

ON THE BLINK
out of order; not working; broken
[descompuesto]
   My car is on the blink. It won't start.

BLOCK

CHIP OFF THE OLD BLOCK
someone who is just like his parents
[alguien que es exactamente como su padre]
   Dan is a great baseball player like his father was; he is a chip off the old block.

BLOOD

BAD* BLOOD
MAKE SOMEONE'S BLOOD BOIL
to make someone very angry
[enfadarle a uno]
   Stories about child abuse make my blood boil.

BLOODY

YELL (SCREAM) BLOODY MURDER
to complain in a loud voice
[quejarse a voz en cuello]
   When the thief grabbed my purse, I yelled bloody murder.

BLOW

BLOW A FUSE (GASKET)
to have an angry outburst
[tener un ataque de furia]
   Jerry blew a fuse when he heard that his employer did not have enough money to pay him his wages.

BLOW HOT AND COLD
to switch from enthusiasm to reluctance, between yes and no; to change one's mind a lot
[vacilar entre el entusiasmo y la duda, entre sí y no]
   John blew hot and cold about taking Lisa to the dance.

BLOW IT
(1) to waste it; squander it; spend it all
[desperdiciarlo; gastarlo todo]
   Alice blew her allowance this week on an expensive box of chocolates.

(2) to make something fail
[fracasar]
   Nancy tried to impress the interviewer, but she blew it when she forgot his name.

BLOW OFF STEAM
to vent one's anger
[aliviar uno su ira]
   Karl felt he was unfairly treated so he blew off steam by running in the park.

BLOW ONE'S MIND
to amaze someone; to be amazed
[asombrar a alguien]
   The thought of winning a free trip to China blew my mind.

BLOW ONE'S STACK
to have an angry outburst
[tener un ataque de furia]
   I blew my stack when I found a $50 ticket on the windshield of my car.

*Look under the **key word*** for this idiom.

BLOWOUT

an expensive meal

[una comida cara]

After the final exam, John and Henry celebrated with a blow-out at the best restaurant in town.

_____

BLOW OVER

to calm down; to subside

[tranquilizarse]

Politicians know that the scandals that interest the public usually blow over in a couple of weeks.

_____

BLOW THE WHISTLE

to report to an authority something that is wrong (usually in the workplace)

[avisar que algo está mal a las autoridades, generalmente en el trabajo]

Ms. Eckstein blew the whistle when she reported to the Equal Opportunities Committee that women were paid lower salaries than other workers .

_____

HAVE A BLOWOUT

to have an auto tire burst suddenly, making the tire flat

[tener un escape rápido de aire de una llanta, con el resultado que la llanta se desinfla]

Jack controlled the car when the tire had a blowout so no one was hurt.

_____

BLUE

BETWEEN THE DEVIL AND THE DEEP BLUE SEA

in a tight spot, in which both choices are bad

[en un dilema, en el cual hay que elegir entre dos males]

Robert was between the devil and the deep blue sea when he had to choose between a job he hated near home, and one he liked that was very far from home.

_____

FEEL BLUE

to feel sad

[sentirse triste]

I feel blue when I think of my girlfriend far away.

_____

ONCE IN A BLUE MOON

seldom; not very often

[raras veces]

I see my cousin Tanya once in a blue moon, perhaps once a year.

_____

OUT OF THE BLUE

suddenly; unexpectedly

[de repente]

There I was, in a restaurant 900 miles from home, and my teacher walked through the door, right out of the blue.

_____

BLUFF

CALL* SOMEONE'S BLUFF

BOARD

BACK* TO THE DRAWING BOARD

BOAT

IN THE SAME BOAT

in the same situation; with the same problem

[en la misma situación; con los mismos problemas]

Rudy and Sam are both in the same boat: failed their final examinations and must repeat the course.

_____

MISS THE BOAT

to lose an opportunity

[perder una oportunidad]

John missed the boat in competing for the art award because he did not submit his work on time.

_____

ROCK THE BOAT

to cause trouble in a peaceful situation

[causar dificultades en una situación apacible]

The waiter gave us a good table in the "No Smoking" section. Don't rock the boat by smoking.

BODY

OVER MY DEAD BODY

absolutely forbidden by me

[sin que yo lo quiera, en absoluto]

She will get that painting over my dead body.

BOGGLE

TO BE MIND-BOGGLING

to overwhelm the mind; be too much for the mind to absorb

[agobiar la imaginación; ser algo demasiado grande para comprender]

The amount of exercise needed to train for the Olympics is mind-boggling.

BOIL

MAKE ONE'S BLOOD* BOIL

BOMBED

BOMBED OUT, BOMBED OUT OF ONE'S MIND OR SKULL

drunk, or drugged

[borracho o narcotizado]

Seth was bombed out because he drank too much beer.

BONE

BONE TO PICK

a point of disagreement; a point to argue or to complain about

[un punto de desacuerdo; algo que discutir]

Lois has a bone to pick with Charlotte, who came late for their appointment.

BONER

PULL A BONER

to do something foolish or stupid

[cometer una tontería]

I pulled a boner when I asked Jim to make a contribution to his own wedding gift.

BONES

FEEL IT IN ONE'S BONES

to have an intuition about something

[tener un presentimiento acerca de algo]

George felt it in his bones that Conrad was going to fail the driving test.

MAKE NO BONES ABOUT

be candid, speak in a direct manner

[hablar francamente]

Bill made no bones about the fact that he did not enjoy opera at all.

BONNET

BEE* IN ONE'S BONNET

BOOB

BOOB-TUBE

television set

[un televisor]

Children spend too many hours watching the boob-tube.

BOOK

CRACK A BOOK

to start to read a book, usually to study

[empezar a leer un libro]

I was so restless that I couldn't even crack a book.

---

*Look under the **key word*** for this idiom.

THROW THE BOOK AT SOMEONE

to punish someone to the full extent permitted
by law

[castigar a alguien con la pena máxima]

> *The judge threw the book at the convicted rapist.*
> *He sentenced him to prison for life.*

```



_____
```

BOOKS

ONE FOR THE BOOKS

outstanding, unusual, memorable

[fuera de serie]

> *That was a great performance. It is one for*
> *the books.*

```



_____
```

BOOM

LOWER THE BOOM ON SOMEONE

to scold or punish someone; discipline someone
for intolerable behavior or actions

[reñir o castigar a alguien]

> *His father lowered the boom on Warren for*
> *misbehaving at the family dinner last week.*

```



_____
```

BOOT

TO BOOT (NOTE: THIS IS NOT A VERB)

in addition

[además]

> *She bought three dresses, and a pair of*
> *slacks to boot.*

```



_____
```

BOSOM

BOSOM FRIEND; BOSOM BUDDY

a very close friend

[un amigo íntimo]

> *Nellie and Gladys have known each other*
> *for years. They are bosom friends.*

```



_____
```

BOTH

BURN THE CANDLE AT BOTH ENDS

to work or socialize without taking a rest

[estar ocupado de día y de noche]

> *He spent all day at the horse races and most of*
> *the night in the nightclub; he was burning the*
> *candle at both ends.*

```



_____
```

BOTTLE

HIT THE BOTTLE

to drink alcoholic beverages to excess

[tomar las bebidas alcohólicas de una manera
excesiva]

> *After he lost his job, Peter hit the bottle.*
> *He is drunk most of the time.*

```



_____
```

BOTTOM

GET TO THE BOTTOM OF SOMETHING

to find the cause or causes of something

[hallar la causa o las causas de algo]

> *I intend to get to the bottom of why Sheila and*
> *Lois are no longer friends.*

```



_____
```

SCRAPE THE BOTTOM OF THE **BARREL***

BRAINSTORM

BRAINSTORM

to think about and discuss a problem (usually in
a group) and list every thought that comes to mind

[debatir un problema, generalmente en un grupo,
y hacer una lista de todos los pensamientos]

> *Our team brainstormed about the project on*
> *China; we came up with some wonderful ideas.*

```



_____
```

BRASS

GET DOWN TO BRASS TACKS

to take care of the details in dealing with a job or
problem

[encargarse uno de los detalles en cuanto a un
trabajo o un problema]

> *Paul had discussed colleges for a long time.*
> *Now he had to get down to brass tacks in filling*
> *out applications.*

```



_____
```

BREAK

BREAK INTO

to enter without permission; enter by force
[entrar sin permiso; entrar con fuerza]

The thieves broke into the bank by drilling their way through walls from the store next door.

BREAK LOOSE

to gain freedom from physical or behavioral restrictions, such as ropes, handcuffs, or prison
[ganar la libertad de restricciones físicas o mentales, como las cuerdas, las esposas,o la cárcel]

John broke loose from the strict rules about how he should dress when he went to college; he wore shorts and a T-shirt to class.

BREAK OFF SOMETHING

to end something (a relationship, or a negotiation)
[romper (una relación o las negociaciónes)]

Mary and Joel quarreled and have decided to break off their engagement to be married.

BREAK ONE'S NECK

to try very hard
[echar muchas esfuerzas]

Murray had to break his neck to get to the meeting on time.

BREAK THE ICE

to create a comfortable atmosphere after initial shyness
[crear un ambiente agradable después de una timidez inicial]

Everyone at the meeting was tense; Sheila broke the ice by telling a joke she had just heard.

BREAK THE NEWS

to announce something for the first time
[dar unas noticias por la primera vez]

Everyone was delighted when Sara broke the news that she was engaged to be married.

GIVE SOMEONE A BREAK; GIVE A BREAK TO SOMEONE

to overlook a rule to help someone
[no hacer caso de una regla, para ayudar a alguien]

I know I'm often late, but I have to get five children off to school. Please give me a break.

MAKE A CLEAN BREAK

to leave, to make a change
[irse, efectuar un cambio]

Jim decided to make a clean break from the work he was doing. He left his job as a salesman, and became a computer programmer.

BREAST

MAKE A CLEAN BREAST

to confess
[confesar]

Jack was ashamed of having hit the child, and he made a clean breast of it to the social worker.

BREATH

SAVE ONE'S BREATH

to stop trying to persuade or reason with someone
[dejar de tratar de razonar con alguien]

He is so hard to convince that you may as well save your breath.

WASTE ONE'S BREATH

to waste one's words; find it useless to explain, talk, argue
[desperdiciar las palabras; encontrarlo inútil explicar, hablar o discutir]

It is a waste of my breath to try to persuade her to vote for my candidate.

17

BREATHE

DON'T BREATHE A WORD

Don't tell someone something. Keep a secret.
[Guarde el secreto. No diga nada a nadie.]
Don't breathe a word about the surprise
party until Monday.

BREEZE

SHOOT THE BREEZE

to chat; converse about matters of no great
importance
[charlar; platicar sobre temas de poca importancia]
I met Betty on the street and we shot the
breeze for a while.

BRICKS

LIKE A TON OF BRICKS

with great force
[con mucho fuerza]
The death of my dog hit me like a ton of bricks.

BRING

BRING DOWN THE HOUSE

to receive a lot of applause
[recibir muchos aplausos]
When Julie Andrews sang in MY FAIR LADY,
she brought down the house.

BRING HOME THE BACON*
BRING TO MIND SOMETHING; BRING SOMETHING TO MIND

to be reminded; to remind one of something
[acordarle a alguien de]
The sight of that bookbag brought to mind the
schoolbag I carried for many years.

BROKE

BE BROKE

to have no money
[no tener dinero]

Larry could not take Jane out to dinner because
he was broke.

BROWN

BROWN BAG*
TO BROWN-NOSE: see APPLE* POLISHER

to seek favor by giving compliments
[ganar los favores de alguien dando complimentos]
Randy is not liked by his fellow workers because
he brown-noses the boss in order to get a promotion.

A BROWN NOSE

one who seeks favor by giving compliments
[el que gana los favores dando complimentos]
Robert always laughs at the teacher's bad jokes;
he is a brown-nose.

BRUSH

BRUSH OFF (GIVE, GET THE)

a disrespectful refusal to deal with someone or
something
[una negativa descortés para no tener que tratar
con una persona]
When James asked Bill for a loan, he got the
brush off.

BRUSH UP ON

to review, to learn again
[repasar, aprender de nuevo]
Before going to France, Amy brushed up
on the French she had learned at school.

BUCK

A BUCK

a dollar
[un dólar]
This watch cost me four hundred bucks.

FAST BUCK

money earned quickly and easily
[dinero ganado con rapidez y facilidad]
Jose thought he could make a fast buck at the race track.

PASS THE BUCK

to shift the responsibility to someone else
[transferir la responsabilidad a otra persona]
Mr. Jones passed the buck for cutting the salaries of his workers. He blamed it on his boss.

THE BUCK STOPS HERE

This person takes the responsibility for whatever has happened.
[está persona acepta la responsabilidad por todo lo que ha sucedido]
Mr. Jones, the head of the company, said, "No matter who caused the accident, the buck stops here, with me."

TO BUCK

to resist, to fight
[resistir a, luchar contra]
I hate to buck the traffic jams on the Expressway.

BUCKET

DROP IN THE BUCKET

an insignificant portion of what is needed
[una parte insignificante de la cantidad necesitada]
I save ten dollars a week to pay for my college education. It is only a drop in the bucket.

KICK THE BUCKET

to die
[morir]
Dan kicked the bucket when he was 55. He left a widow and one child.

BUCKLE

BUCKLE DOWN

to settle down, to get to work
[tranquilizarse; empezar a trabajar]
When she knew that going to college depended on her exam grades, Sabina buckled down and studied.

BUD

NIP SOMETHING IN THE BUD

to stop a program or activity just as it is beginning
[hacer parar un programa o una actividad precisamente cuando está comenzando]
When Sophie learned about the plans to give her a big party, she nipped the whole thing in the bud. She said she was going to be out of town.

BUDDY-BUDDY

BUDDY-BUDDY

very friendly
[muy amistoso]
Tina and Nancy are always together; they are buddy-buddy.

BUG

BUG

to listen in to (and sometimes tape) telephone conversations without permission
[escuchar (y a veces grabar en cinta) conversaciones telefónicas sin permiso]
Many persons worry about their telephones being bugged because it is an invasion of their privacy.

BUG OFF!

Go away. Leave me alone.
[¡Lárguese! ¡Déjeme en paz!]
Bug off; You are annoying me.

*Look under the **key word*** for this idiom.

PUT A BUG IN SOMEONE'S EAR
to give someone an idea
[darle a alguien una idea]
> *He put a bug in my ear about entering the ice-skating contest.*

BUG SOMEONE (NEGATIVE: STOP BUGGING SOMEONE)
to annoy someone repeatedly (See BUG OFF)
[dejar de molestarle a alguien (vease BUG OFF)]
> *Julius was annoyed by Jim's asking him again and again for the money he owed him ; He told Jim to stop bugging him.*

BULL
BULL IN A CHINA SHOP
a person who is clumsy, accident prone, with a tendency to break things
[una persona torpe e inclinada a causar accidentes, dispuesto a romper cosas]
> *David dropped his tea cup, and also knocked down Nancy's cup. He was like a bull in a china shop.*

COCK* AND BULL STORY

TAKE THE BULL BY THE HORNS
to deal with a challenge directly
[encarar un reto directamente]
> *Kim, after many hours of discussion, finally took the bull by the horns and asked her employer for a raise in pay.*

BULLET
BITE THE BULLET
to do what has to be done even if it is unpleasant or painful
[hacer lo que se debe hacer, hasta si resulta desagradable o doloroso]
> *I postponed going to the dentist many times, but I finally bit the bullet and went.*

BULLETS
SWEAT BULLETS
to be apprehensive of, or experience something uncomfortable or fearful
[estar temeroso o experimentar algo incómodo o espantoso]
> *Joe sweat bullets while waiting for the jury's verdict.*

BUM
BUM AROUND
to wander around aimlessly
[errar sin objeto]
> *Tom had three hours with nothing to do, so he bummed around downtown.*

GIVE SOMEONE THE BUM'S RUSH
to force someone to leave quickly
[obligar a alguien que se vaya rápidamente]
> *The waiter probably needs this table for others; he is giving us the bum's rush.*

BUM TICKER
a defective heart
[un corazón defectuoso]
> *After his heart attack, Evan was afraid to lift the heavy box because of his bum ticker.*

BUMP
BUMP OFF SOMEONE; BUMP SOMEONE OFF
to murder, to kill
[asesinar]
> *This man is dangerous; they say he has bumped off three people.*

SIT THERE LIKE A BUMP ON A LOG
to be unresponsive
[estar impasible]
> *Don't sit there like a bump on a log. Help me lift this trunk.*

_____

BUNDLE

MAKE A BUNDLE
to earn a lot of money
[ganar mucho dinero]
> *Ron's friends helped him make a bundle on a stock trade.*

_____

BURN

BURN A HOLE IN ONE'S POCKET
to have money that one is eager to spend
[dishacerse de algo, generalmente el dinero, de buena gana]
> *He spent so much on his clothes, it seemed as if money was burning a hole in his pocket.*

_____

BURN ONESELF OUT, TO BE BURNED OUT
to be exhausted because of emotional and physical pressure at work
[estar agotado a causa de las presiones emocionales y físicas en el trabajo]
> *Tanya, the social worker, retired early. She was burned out after working for 10 years with Alzheimer disease patients.*

_____

BURN THE CANDLE AT **BOTH*** ENDS

BURNED

BURN*ED OUT

GET BURNED
to suffer unpleasant consequences
[sufrir consecuencias desagradables]
> *When I played in the stock market, I got burned twice, and then I quit.*

_____

BURST

BURST INTO TEARS
to start crying
[deshacerse en lágrimas]
> *Manya burst into tears when she heard that her mother was dying.*

_____

BURST OUT CRYING
SEE **BURST INTO TEARS**

BURST OUT LAUGHING
to start laughing
[reventar de risa]
> *Sonia burst out laughing when she saw my funny dress.*

_____

BURY

BURY THE HATCHET
to make peace
[establecer la paz]
> *After an argument, the two sisters did not speak to each other for years; finally they buried the hatchet, and they now are friends.*

_____

BUSH

BEAT* AROUND THE BUSH

BUSHED

BUSHED
tired; exhausted
[rendido]
> *I've been packing these cartons all day. I am bushed!*

_____

BUSINESS

MEAN BUSINESS
to be serious about something; to intend to do what one says
[estar serio sobre algo; hablar en serio sobre un tema, sobre el cual uno piensa hacer algo]
> *We though Alan was joking about cutting off his son's allowance, but he meant business.*

*Look under the **key word*** for this idiom.

MIND* ONE'S BUSINESS
MONKEY* BUSINESS

BUTT

BUTT IN

to interrupt; to intrude

[interrumpir; entremeterse]

Every time I speak to my friend, my sister butts in.

BUTT OUT

not to intrude on a problem or situation; to remove oneself

[no entremeterse uno en un problema o una situación; retirarse]

Tom's father told him to butt out of Angelo's dispute with Rudolpho.

BUTTER

BUTTER UP TO SOMEONE

to try to get special treatment from someone by complimenting and doing favors for that person

[tratar de conseguir tratamiento especial de alguien por medio de halagarlo y hacerle favores especiales]

Mary brought a newspaper every day for her supervisor. By buttering up to him, she hoped for a raise in pay.

BUTTINSKY

BUTTINSKY (A)

one who interrupts, intrudes

[una persona que se entremete]

Nadya is involved in everybody's affairs; she is a buttinsky.

BUTTON

BUTTON ONE'S LIP

to keep a secret; not to reveal something

[no divulgar un secreto]

Harris told Unger about his love for Sonia, and since no one else knew, Unger was asked to button his lip.

BUY

BUY A PIG IN A POKE

to buy something without seeing it or having a full description of it

[comprar una cosa sin verla o tener una descripción completa de ella]

I had no time to shop around for a used car; I bought this one without driving it; it was like buying a pig in a poke.

BYGONES

LET BYGONES BE BYGONES

to forget and forgive what has happened in the past

[olvidar y perdonar lo que ocurrió en el pasado]

The brothers, who had been angry with each other for three years, met last week and agreed to let bygones be bygones.

CADET

SPACE* CADET

CAIN

RAISE CAIN

to make a big fuss

[armar un jaleo]

Leonard raised Cain when he was told that the laundry had misplaced his shirts.

CAKE

A PIECE OF CAKE

something easy

[algo fácil]

I finished today's homework in ten minutes; it was a piece of cake.

HAVE ONE'S CAKE AND EAT IT TOO (EAT ONE'S CAKE AND HAVE IT TOO)

to seek two desirable outcomes, when choosing one usually makes the other impossible

[querer sacar un provecho de dos circunstancias opuestas, cuando el uno hace imposible de ségundo]

Harry wanted to eat his cake and have it too by remaining engaged to Jane and going out with Jane's roommate, Phyllis.

TAKE THE CAKE

to be outstanding, win the prize

[ser fuera de serie]

Tina's story about her trip to New York takes the cake. It was written up in the newspaper.

CALL

AT ONE'S **BECK*** AND CALL

CALL IT A DAY

to stop doing something for that day

[terminar uno su trabajo para el resto del día]

Jake shovelled the snow for four hours; he was exhausted and called it a day.

CALL IT QUITS

to stop, finish, quit a project

[terminar un proyecto]

I tried all day to repair the sink, but finally I had to call it quits.

CALL SOMEONE ON THE CARPET

to summon someone for criticism or punishment for undesirable behavior

[mandar que alguien se presente para una crítica o un castigo por comportamiento incorrecto]

Betty's supervisor called her on the carpet for being late at work three days in a row.

CALL SOMEONE'S BLUFF

to require someone to prove his/her unproved statement

[exigirle a alguien que compruebe una declaración no comprobada]

Myra said she would have me fired if I did not do what she said. I called her bluff — and I was not fired.

CALL THE SHOTS

to be in command; to be in a position of power; to direct

[estar encargado; tener la autoridad]

The coach calls the shots on that team.

CALL UP SOMETHING; CALL SOMETHING UP

(1) to call someone on the telephone

[telefonearle a alguien]

*Look under the **key word*** for this idiom.

Stuart's mother called him up every day.

_____

(2) to retrieve information from memory or from a computer file

[recoger información de la memoria de una computadora]

Jennie asked if the computer could call up the names and addresses of the girls in her graduation class.

_____

(3) to request a person or persons to appear

[pedir que se presente una persona]

The courtroom clerk called up six people to be interviewed as possible jurors for the next trial.

_____

CLOSE CALL

narrow escape from danger

[un escape del peligro]

When the hammer fell off the ladder, it missed Tom's head by one inch. That was a close call.

_____

CALLING

THE POT CALLING THE KETTLE BLACK

calling someone a name that also describes oneself

[denunciar uno a otra persona por ser lo que es él mismo]

The high-priced furniture dealer said that the automobile shop charged very high prices. It was the pot calling the kettle black.

_____

CAN

BEFORE YOU CAN SAY JACK ROBINSON

very quickly

[muy rápidamente]

The magician brought the rabbit out of the hat before you could say Jack Robinson.

_____

CATCH AS CATCH CAN

to use whatever is available; in an irregular manner

[utilizar lo que esté a la mano; al azar]

Since we had no time to shop, we used whatever was in the refrigerator and made dinner catch as catch can.

_____

TO BE CANNED

to be dismissed or fired

[ser despedido]

Imry knew that if he was late one more time, he would be canned.

_____

TO CAN SOMEONE OR SOMETHING

(1) to dismiss (fire) from a position;

[despedir a alquien de su empleo]

The fifth time Jorge came late to work, the foreman canned him

(2) to preserve fruits or vegetables in a jar or can

[conservar frutas o verduras en un pote]

My mother cans delicious peaches and apples every year.

_____

CANDLE

BURN THE CANDLE AT **BOTH*** ENDS

CAN'T HOLD A CANDLE TO

to be inferior to

[ser menos bueno que]

Angela's performance was good, but it can't hold a candle to that of Julie Andrews.

_____

CANNED

TO BE **CAN***NED

CAP

A FEATHER IN ONE'S CAP

a victory; an achievement in which one may take pride

[un éxito de que uno puede estar orgulloso]

Winning the math medal was a feather in Martha's cap.

CARDS

LAY (PUT) ONE'S CARDS ON THE TABLE

to be honest; to reveal everthing

[ser sincero; revelar todo]

Abby told the salesman exactly how much money he could spend. He laid his cards on the table.

CARPET

CALL* ON THE CARPET

CARRIED

BE (GET) CARRIED AWAY

to have an overwhelming emotional reaction to an event, usually with joy

[estar arrebatado]

Joan was so eager to have a child; when she learned that she was pregnant, she was carried away with joy.

CARRY

CARRY ON

to continue what one is doing; to continue a project

[continuar uno lo que hace]

Josephine carried on the family business after her parents died.

CARRY THE BALL*

CART

PUT THE CART BEFORE THE HORSE

to do things backwards

[hacer las cosas al revés]

Alice put the cart before the horse by signing the contract to buy the house before she discovered she did not have the money for the deposit.

UPSET THE APPLE CART

to disrupt the established order or plan

[estorbar el orden establecido]

Dan upset the apple cart by delivering the flyers two days after they were supposed to be handed out.

CASE

CASE THE JOINT*

MAKE A FEDERAL CASE OUT OF SOMETHING

to exaggerate the importance of an event; to do something out of proportion to its importance

[exagerar la importancia de un evento]

Mama made a federal case out of it when I lost my mittens.

OPEN* AND SHUT CASE

CAT

FAT CAT

one who prospers and has many advantages, earned through his position rather than his work

[uno que prospera y goza de muchas ventajas ganadas mas por su rango que por su trabájo]

The Mayor's assistant is chauffeured in a Rolls Royce everywhere he goes. He is a fat cat.

GRIN LIKE A CHESHIRE CAT

to smile broadly

[dar uno una sonrisa grande]

Mimi grinned from ear to ear like a Cheshire cat when she ate that ice cream cone.

*Look under the **key word*** for this idiom.

LET THE CAT OUT OF THE **BAG***

CATCH
CATCH-AS-CATCH-**CAN***

CATCH FIRE
> (1) to start to burn
> [prender fuego]
>> *Rags soaked in oil catch fire very quickly.*

_____

> (2) to suddenly become important
> [ganar importancia de repente]
>> *Mary's idea to sell home baked cakes to raise money caught fire. Now everyone bakes cakes for the fund-raiser.*

_____

CATCH ON
> to understand
> [comprender]
>> *Rudy learns very easily; he catches on quickly.*

_____

CATCH ONE'S EYE
> to get someone's attention
> [llamarle a uno la atención]
>> *The pearl necklace in the jewelry shop window caught my eye.*

_____

CATCH SOMEONE RED*-HANDED

CATCH 22
> a situation which cannot be resolved because each rule makes another rule impossible to follow
> [una situación que no se puede resolver porque las reglas se contradicen]
>> *John said he wanted to be married. Grace wants to marry John. John thinks poorly of himself. He feels that anyone who wants to marry him has poor judgement. So he rejects Grace. They are in a catch 22 situation.*

_____

CATCH UP
> to overtake
> [alcanzar]
>> *Samantha started the race slowly, but she quickly caught up to the leading runner.*

_____

CATS
RAIN CATS AND DOGS
> to rain very heavily
> [llover a cántaros]
>> *When I left the subway, it rained cats and dogs. My shoes were completely soaked when I got home.*

_____

CAUGHT
BE CAUGHT SHORT
> to have an insufficient supply
> [tener provisiones insuficientes]
>> *With only two stoves left in the store, Tim was caught short; he had orders to deliver ten stoves stoves the next day.*

_____

CEILING
HIT THE CEILING (ROOF)
> to become very angry
> [enfurecerse]
>> *The electric bill was very high in January. John hit the ceiling when he received it.*

_____

CENTS
FEEL LIKE TWO CENTS
> to feel humiliated
> [sentir humillado]
>> *When the teacher announced that I had failed the final examination, I felt like two cents.*

_____

PUT IN ONE'S TWO CENTS' WORTH
> to add one's opinion, or to add some comments
> [dar uno su opinión o unos comentarios]

When the men discussed women's rights, I put in my two cents' worth, and suggested that women be invited.

This automobile has had many owners; now that I have purchased it, it has changed hands again.

CHAIN
CHAIN SMOKER
one who smokes one cigarette right after another
[fumador en cadena]
Doctors remind us that chain smokers usually develop lung cancer.

CHALK
CHALK UP
to score
[ganar]
Brazil chalked up another victory in soccer. They won the world cup for the fourth time.

CHANCE
NOT TO HAVE A GHOST OF A CHANCE
to have no opportunity, or only a slight possibility
[no tener ninguna oportunidad, o tener la más mínima]
He hasn't a ghost of a chance of winning that contest.

SNOWBALL'S CHANCE IN HELL (TO HAVE A)
to have no chance at all
[no tener ninguna oportunidad]
Zoe has a snowball's chance in hell of winning a scholarship because her grades are so low.

STAND* A CHANCE

CHANGE
CHANGE HANDS
to transfer control or ownership from one to another
[transferir uno el control o la propiedad de una persona a otra]

CHANGE ONE'S MIND
to alter one's opinion or decision.
[cambiar uno de opinión]
We hope that Jerry will change his mind about voting against abortion.

CHANNELS
GO THROUGH CHANNELS
to go through the proper procedures, step by step
[pasar por los trámites de costumbre, paso a paso]
It was important to go through channels when complaining about pollution in the workplace.

CHARGE
GET A CHARGE (KICK, BANG*) OUT OF IT
TAKE CHARGE
to take control of something or someone
[asumir uno el control sobre algo o alguien]
When the babysitter arrived, she took charge of Bobby.

CHASE
A WILD GOOSE CHASE
an impossible, very difficult, or fruitless investigation or pursuit
[una investigación o búsqueda sin éxito]
With no clues, Tom's hunt for his lost dog proved to be a wild goose chase.

CHECK
DOUBLE*-CHECK

CHECKUP
A CHECKUP

an examination, usually medical, but also for an automobile or equipment
[un examen físico de una persona, o mecánico de un coche o una máquina]

> *Doctors recommend a full medical checkup once a year.*

CHEEK

TONGUE IN CHEEK

spoken with a serious tone, though making a joke; not meant seriously
[hablado de una manera seria, aunque con la intención de chiste]

> *Tongue in cheek, I told Abner that we had not left any birthday cake for him. He thought I was serious and got very upset.*

CHESHIRE

GRIN LIKE A CHESHIRE CAT*

CHEST

GET SOMETHING OFF ONE'S CHEST

to tell something that has been on one's mind
[expresar uno algo que ha había pensado]

> *I finally got it off my chest. I told Susanne I was worried about her threat to quit her job.*

CHEW

BITE* OFF MORE THAN ONE CAN CHEW
CHEW ONE'S EAR*
CHEW THE FAT*

CHICKENS

COUNT ONE'S CHICKENS BEFORE THEY ARE HATCHED

to plan to use something before one has it
[pensar uno usar algo sin tenerlo todavia]

> *Doris counted her chickens before they were hatched when she spent the money she thought she would inherit from her aunt, but didn't.*

CHILL

CHILL OUT
SEE BUTT* OUT

CHILLING

SPINE*-CHILLING

CHIN

KEEP ONE'S CHIN UP

to be brave, to hope for the best
[ser valiente, anticipar lo mejor]

> *Lotte was worried about her family in Bosnia. But she kept her chin up, hoping that they were safe.*

CHINA

BULL* IN A CHINA SHOP

CHIP

CHIP OFF THE OLD BLOCK*

to have a chip on one's shoulder
to be ready to pick a quarrel with little provocation
[estar uno listo de pelear sin mucho motivo]

> *It is difficult to converse with Abby because I never know what will make him angry. He always has a chip on his shoulder.*

CHIPS

BE IN THE CHIPS

to have a lot of money
[tener mucho dinero]

> *Betty won the lottery; now she is in the chips.*

LET THE CHIPS FALL WHERE THEY MAY

to do something, regardless of the consequences
[hacer algo sin pensar en las consecuencias]

> *The director forbade all smoking in the factory. He knew it would cause trouble, but he let the chips fall where they may.*

WHEN THE CHIPS ARE DOWN

when a serious condition exists
[en caso de una situación grave]

> *When the chips are down, Jim will be there to help his sister.*

CIRCLES

RUN AROUND IN CIRCLES

to repeat the same failed attempts to solve a problem

[repetir los mismos recursos fracasados para tratar de resolver un problema]

Without the missing information, we could not solve the problem. We kept running around in circles.

CLAM

CLAM UP

to refuse to talk

[rehusar de hablar]

When Rodney was questioned about the robbery, he clammed up.

CLAMP

CLAMP DOWN ON

to enforce the rules; to restrict

[enforzar las reglas; restringir]

The police have clamped down on beggars in the subway.

CLEAN

CLEAN BILL* OF HEALTH

CLEAN SOMEONE OUT

to take everything away from someone

[quitarle uno todo a alguien]

He had no money with which to start a new business after his partner cleaned him out.

COME CLEAN

to confess

[confesar]

The congressman finally came clean about taking a bribe.

KEEP ONE'S NOSE CLEAN

to keep out of trouble

[mantenerse uno libre de dificultades]

While the others were messing around with drugs, Paul kept his nose clean.

MAKE* A CLEAN BREAK

MAKE* A CLEAN BREAST

CLEANERS

TAKE SOMEONE TO THE CLEANERS

to take most of someone's possessions

[quitarle uno a alguien la mayoría de sus posesiones]

The experienced gambler took the young card players to the cleaners. He left them with no money.

CLEAR

CLEAR OUT

to leave; to take things out of a place

[irse; sacar las cosas de un lugar]

Mr. Jones did not like his tenant; he asked him to clear out of the apartment.

CLEAR THE AIR*

MAKE CLEAR; MAKE SOMETHING CLEAR

to explain

[aclarar]

The new physics teacher made it clear that test scores were only part of the final grade.

STEER CLEAR OF SOMEONE

to avoid someone

[evitar a alguien]

Jamie steered clear of her old boy friend in the school yard.

THE COAST IS CLEAR

There is no one and nothing in the way.

[No hay moros.]

They looked both ways before crossing the street and saw that the coast was clear.

*Look under the **key word*** for this idiom.

Joe has been working around the clock since he opened his fruit market.

CLIMB

CLIMB ON THE **BANDWAGON***

CLINK

IN THE CLINK

in prison

[en la cárcel]

It is shocking to hear that Sam was in the clink overnight because he was not wearing his seat belt while driving.

CLIP

CLIP JOINT

a place of business that charges too much

[un negocio que cobra demasiado]

This clip joint charges five dollars for a cup of coffee.

CLOBBER

CLOBBER SOMEONE

to beat up someone; to beat someone

[pegarle a alguien]

Kent clobbered his little brother every time he passed by.

CLOCK

CLOCK-WATCHER

one who is careful not to work longer than the required time

[alguien que se ocupa de mirar el reloj para no trabajar más de lo que es el requisito]

Ann was completely absorbed in her work and often worked late, while Daisy was a clock-watcher and left promptly at 5 every day.

WORK AROUND THE CLOCK

to work long hours, many days a week

[trabajar horas largas, muchos días a la semana]

CLOSE

CLOSE **CALL***

CLOSE SHAVE

a narrow escape from danger

[por poco tener uno un accidente o una experiencia mala]

That automobile missed hitting me by two inches. That was a close shave.

CLOSET

COME OUT OF THE CLOSET

to announce that one is gay or homosexual

[declarar uno ser homosexual]

Though he had been nervous about it, Barry's coworkers were courteous and warm when he came out of the closet.

HAVE A SKELETON IN THE CLOSET

to have an embarrassing secret

[tener un secreto humillante]

Mr. Smith will not run for election because he has too many skeletons in the closet.

CLOTHESHORSE

CLOTHESHORSE

one who takes excessive pride in clothing and wears different clothes for each occasion

[una persona que se enorgullece de su ropa y que luce distin ta ropa en cada ocasión]

Reggie is a clotheshorse. I wonder how much time and money she spends on her clothing,

CLOTHING

WOLF IN SHEEP'S CLOTHING

a dangerous person posing as someone peaceful and innocent

*Look under the **key word*** for this idiom.

30

[una persona peligrosa disfrazada como persona apacible e inocente]

The drug pusher was dressed like a clown and was giving out free samples of chewing gum that contained cocaine. He was a wolf in sheep's clothing.

_____

CLOUDS

HAVE ONE'S HEAD IN THE CLOUDS

to daydream; to be impractical; to be lost in thought

[tener uno la cabeza en las nubes]

Martha had her head in the clouds when she tripped in the street and broke her ankle.

_____

CLOUT

HAVE CLOUT (PULL, CLOUT, AN IN)

to have an advantage, to have power

[tener la ventaja, tener autoridad]

When Paul told the bookstore owners to lower their prices, they did. Paul is the school principal, and he has clout.

_____

CLOVER

BE IN CLOVER

to be in a good situation, particularly with money

[en una buena situación, especialmente en cuanto al dinero]

Since she inherited her aunt's money, Gloria has been in clover.

_____

CLUE

CLUE SOMEONE IN

to give a hint

[darle a alguien una pista]

At the treasure hunt, the children wanted to be clued in to where the prize was hidden.

_____

COALS

HAUL (RAKE) OVER THE COALS

to scold severely

[reñir con severidad]

Mom hauled (raked) me over the coals when I came home at two o'clock in the morning.

_____

COAST

THE COAST IS **CLEAR***

COCK

COCK AND BULL STORY

a story that is not true

[una historia inventada]

He tells a cock and bull story about his being a champion ice skater.

_____

COLD

BLOW* HOT AND COLD

COLD TURKEY

stopping an addictive habit all at once

[dejar de tomar las drogas de súbito]

This is his first week without drugs; he stopped cold turkey.

_____

GET THE COLD SHOULDER

to be ignored by someone

[ser ignorado o rechazado]

Sam got the cold shoulder when he asked Susan to dance.

_____

GIVE THE COLD SHOULDER

to ignore someone

[ignorar uno a otro]

Stella gave a cold shoulder to the reporter who had criticized her.

_____

HAVE COLD **FEET***

THROW COLD WATER ON

to discourage

[desanimarle a uno]

*Look under the **key word*** for this idiom.

Deirdre threw cold water on our plans to go to the circus.

COLLAR

GET HOT UNDER THE COLLAR

to get angry

[enojarse]

I got hot under the collar when she got in front of me on the line waiting for the bus.

COLOR

HORSE OF ANOTHER COLOR

a different view of something or someone; a different thing altogether

[otro punto de vista hacia algo o alguien; cosa enteramente distinta]

I thought we were talking about a young person wanting a chair to rest on. If she is 80 years old, that is a horse of a different color.

COLORS

COME THROUGH (PASS) WITH FLYING COLORS

to be outstandingly successful

[tener un éxito extraordinario]

She got an A in every course. She came through with flying colors.

COMB

WITH A FINE-TOOTHED COMB

very carefully

[con mucho cuidado]

I can't find my key to the garage. I have gone through every room in the house with a fine-toothed comb.

COME

COME **APART*** AT THE SEAMS

COME **CLEAN***

COME DOWN HARD ON SOMEONE

to give someone severe punishment

[darle a alguien un castigo duro]

The teacher came down hard on Sheldon for cheating on the examination. She failed him in the course.

COME HELL OR HIGH WATER

no matter what happens

[pase lo que pase]

I will attend graduation come hell or high water.

COME IN HANDY

to be useful

[ser útil]

This broom will come in handy when I need to sweep the porch.

COME OFF IT

to stop pretending; to stop joking

[dejar de fingir]

Angela told Ronnie to come off it; his joking was not appropriate at this serious time.

COME OUT OF THE **CLOSET***

COME TO THE END OF ONE'S ROPE

to reach the límits of one's ability to cope with a situation

[llegar a los límites de poder aguantar una situación]

Gordon has no more sandbags to keep out the flood at his home on the Mississippi shore. He is now at the end of his rope.

COME THROUGH WITH FLYING **COLORS***

TILL THE **COWS*** COME HOME

COMING

HAVE IT COMING

to deserve something, usually a punishment, but sometimes a reward

[merecer algo, generalmente un castigo, pero también un premio]

Paul caught a bad cold. He had it coming; I had urged him to wear his raincoat, but he refused.

NOT TO KNOW IF ONE IS COMING OR GOING

to be confused

[estar uno confuso]

I am so exhausted that I don't know whether I am coming or going.

COMPANY

KEEP SOMEONE COMPANY

to stay with someone, usually to keep that person from being lonely

[acompañar uno a alguien, usualmente para evitar que se sienta solitario]

I kept Tim company on his walk to the train.

COMPLIMENT

PAY A LEFT-HANDED COMPLIMENT

to give a compliment that really is an insult

[dar un piropo que en realidad es un insulto]

When Laura wore the new dress, Nancy paid her the left-handed compliment of saying that she looked better that night than she usually did.

CONK

CONK OUT

to break down; to be unable to do its work

[fallar; ser uno incapaz de hacer su trabajo]

Just as we were leaving to go to the airport, the car conked out.

CONNIPTIONS

HAVE CONNIPTIONS

to become hysterical

[ponerse agitado]

He had conniptions when he was told he could not go to the baseball game.

COOK

COOK SOMEONE'S GOOSE

to hurt or ruin someone

[dañar o arruinar a alguien]

Peter cooked his own goose by getting to work late every day. He was fired.

COOL

COOL AS A CUCUMBER

calm, relaxed, not excited

[tranquilo]

She was cool as a cucumber, even though it was her first time on TV.

COOL IT

to relax; not to be excited

[calmarse]

Ken told Bob to cool it; they were in no danger, and being excited would not be helpful.

LOSE ONE'S COOL

to become excited

[ponerse agitado]

He lost his cool when he discovered that his wallet was missing.

COOP

FLY THE COOP

leave; disappear

[irse; desaparecer]

Carlo flew the coop, instead of appearing at his trial for robbery.

33

COP

COP OUT

an excuse for taking no responsibility

[un pretexto para no aceptar responsabilidad]

Noel said he could not help us move because he had twisted his ankle. That was an easy cop-out.

COP-OUT

to evade responsibility

[evadir un deber]

Ned copped out on his promise to clean up after the party;he said he had a headache, and left early.

CORNERS

CUT CORNERS

to eliminate details in order to do something quickly or cheaply

[eliminar los pormenores para hacer algo rápidamente o económicamenté]

Her work was always done carefully and in great detail; she never cut corners.

COST

COST AN **ARM*** AND A LEG

COUGH

COUGH UP SOMETHING

(1) to pay someone unwillingly

[pagarle uno a alguien de mala gana]

Do you think you can cough up the fifty dollars you owe me?

(2) to expel (spit out) by coughing

[gargajear]

Marie is not feeling well, and can't hold her food. She coughs it up every time she eats.

COUNT

COUNT ON SOMEONE

to rely on someone

[contar con alguien]

Can I count on you to help clean out the attic?

COUNT YOUR **CHICKENS*** BEFORE THEY ARE HATCHED

COVER

COVER A LOT OF GROUND

to accomplish a lot; do a big job

[lograr mucho]

Your essay on Bosnia discussed the leaders as well as the battles. You cover a lot of ground.

COVER FOR SOMEONE

(1) to protect someone

[proteger a alguien]

Joe covered for John, saying they had been together when the crime occurred.

(2) to substitute for someone in a particular situation

[sustituir a alguien; reemplazar a alguien]

The night that Susie could not work, Anne covered for her.

COVERUP

alibi

[una coartada]

They did not want anyone to know that they broke into the office, and so they arranged a cover-up.

COWS

TILL THE COWS COME HOME

a long time, perhaps forever

[mucho tiempo, posiblemente la eternidad]
She does his errands so slowly that you will not see him again until the cows come home.

```
_____
_____
```

CRACK

CRACK A **BOOK***

CRACK A JOKE

to say something funny
[decir algo chistoso]
Dan is never serious; he is always cracking a joke.

```
_____
_____
```

CRACK DOWN ON

to take harsh measures against
[tomar medidas contra desagradables]
The government is cracking down on drugs.

```
_____
_____
```

HARD (TOUGH) NUT TO CRACK

(1) a problem that is difficult to solve
[un problema que es difícil de resolver]
Repairing this computer is a tough nut to crack.

```
_____
_____
```

(2) a person whom it is hard to get to agree
[una persona con quién es difícil estar de acuerdo]
Getting permission from the foreman to leave early is almost impossible. He is a hard nut to crack.

```
_____
_____
```

TAKE A CRACK AT DOING SOMETHING

to try to
[tratar de]
I took a crack at learning to play bridge, but with no success.

```
_____
_____
```

CRAZY

DRIVE SOMEONE CRAZY (INSANE)

to make someone lose one's mind
[volverle a uno loco]
She nags me so much that she drives me crazy (insane).

```
_____
_____
```

CREAM

CREAM OF THE CROP

the best of something
[la flor y nata]
This book is good. In fact, it is the cream of the crop this year.

```
_____
_____
```

CREEK

UP A CREEK

in a bad situation
[en malas circunstancias]
I've lost my job, and now I'm up a creek.

```
_____
_____
```

CROCODILE

CROCODILE TEARS

false tears; insincere sympathy
[lágrimas falsas; compasión fingida]
Minnie wept crocodile tears at her neighbor's funeral. Actually, she did not like the woman.

```
_____
_____
```

CROOK

BY HOOK OR BY CROOK

by whatever means are necessary to do something.
[a buenas o a malas]
I plan to get the best grade in my studies by hook or by crook.

```
_____
_____
```

CROP

CREAM* OF THE CROP

*Look under the **key word*** for this idiom.

CROSS

CROSS ONE'S MIND

to have a brief thought

[ocurrírsele a alguien; cruzar por la mente]

It crossed my mind that we had an appointment this afternoon, but then I forgot it.

```
_____
_____
```

DOUBLE-CROSS

to betray someone

[traicionar uno a alguien]

John double crossed Philipe when he told the police that Philipe was the driver of the car that was used in the robbery.

```
_____
_____
```

CROSSED

KEEP ONE'S FINGERS CROSSED

to wish for good luck, or for something to go well

[desear buena fortuna, o que salga algo bien]

When Stella went for her medical examination, I kept my fingers crossed.

```
_____
_____
```

CROW

AS THE CROW FLIES

the direct distance

[por la ruta más directa]

From Boston to NY it is 200 miles as the crow flies; by car it is 230 miles.

```
_____
_____
```

EAT CROW

to be humiliated by admitting one was wrong

[estar uno humillado por confesar que se había equivocado]

Jack ate crow when he had to confess to his friends that he had lied about having a college degree.

```
_____
_____
```

CRUSH

HAVE A CRUSH ON SOMEONE

to be infatuated with someone

[estar infatuado de]

Many girls had a crush on Elvis Presley.

```
_____
_____
```

CRY

CRY (SAY) "UNCLE"

to say "I give up" or "I yield" under pressure, usually physical

[rendirse]

He twisted my arm until I cried "uncle".

```
_____
_____
```

CRY WOLF

to make a false alarm; ask for help when it is not needed

[gritar "El lobo"]

Sheila called the doctor for every small pain. Then when she was really in great pain, the doctor was not worried. She had cried wolf too often.

```
_____
_____
```

A FAR CRY FROM

very different from

[muy diferente de]

Her simple hairdo now is a far cry from the bouffant hairdo she had last year.

```
_____
_____
```

CRYING

BURST* OUT CRYING

CUCUMBER

COOL* AS A CUCUMBER

CUE

CUE SOMEONE IN

to give suggestions and information relating to a problem

[dar sugerencias e información sobre un problema]

I asked them to cue me in on how to find a good physician while traveling.

```
_____
_____
```

*Look under the **key word*** for this idiom.

CUP

ONE'S CUP OF TEA

something one prefers

[lo que uno prefiere]

Teaching English is easy. It is my cup of tea.

_____
_____

CURTAIN

IRON CURTAIN

the phantom curtain between Eastern and Western block nations before the dissolution of the former Soviet Union

[la Cortina de Hierro]

It is a relief to the whole world that the Iron Curtain between the Soviet Union and the West no longer exists.

_____
_____

CURVE

THROW SOMEONE A CURVE BALL

to confuse someone by doing something unexpected

[confundir a alguien haciendo lo inesperado]

Suddenly Bill asked Tom to give a lecture on AIDS. Tom was unprepared; that was throwing him a curve ball.

_____
_____

CUT

BE CUT OUT TO BE

to be destined to be

[ser destinado a ser]

This five year old is very graceful. He seems cut out to be a dancer.

_____
_____

CUT CORNERS*

CUT DOWN ON SOMETHING

to take less of something

[tomar una cantidad reducida]

Judy has cut down on sweets because of her diabetes.

_____
_____

CUT SOMEONE DOWN TO SIZE; SOMEONE CUT DOWN TO SIZE

to reduce someone's feeling of superiority

[disminuirle a alguien sus sentimientos de superioridad]

Lily was cut down to size when she saw how many classmates got higher grades than she did on the final exam.

_____
_____

DALLY

DILLY*-DALLY

DAMPER

PUT A DAMPER ON

to discourage

[desanimar]

Our daughter's illness put a damper on our plans to travel to Yellowstone this summer.

_____
_____

DANCE

SONG AND DANCE

a set of explanations and excuses that is used again and again

[las explicaciones y las excusas que se emplean una y otra vez]

When asked about the cast on her arm, Lulu went into her song and dance about some accident.

_____
_____

DARK

DARK HORSE

a candidate for office who is not well known

[un candidato político poco conocido]

The leading candidates had so many scandals in their history that the party leaders decided to nominate a dark horse.

_____
_____

DATE

BLIND* DATE

OUT OF DATE

no longer fashionable

[pasado de moda]

My high-heeled shoes of 1940 are now out of date.

TO DATE
until now
[hasta el presente]
Mary owes Jane $27 to date.

UP TO DATE
fashionable
[de moda]
Nowadays, sneakers are up to date on almost any occasion.

DAWN

DAWN ON
to become clear to
[ocurrirsele a (una idea)]
Nobody seemed to be going to school, and it suddenly dawned on me that it was a school holiday.

DAY

CALL* IT A DAY

DAY IN, DAY OUT
every day
[día tras día]
Dan ate the same breakfast, day in, day out.

RED LETTER DAY
(1) special day of celebration
[día de fiesta]
Our family has a red letter day on my grandmother's birthday.

(2) special sale day
[día especial para las gangas]
The Bloom Department Store has a red letter day once a month.

DAYLIGHT

SEE DAYLIGHT
to know that the solution to the problem is very near
[saber que la resolución de un problema está muy cerca]
Neal had been saving money for 9 months to pay off a debt. He needs only twenty dollars more, and he now sees daylight.

DAYLIGHTS

SCARE THE DAYLIGHTS OUT OF SOMEONE
to frighten someone
[espantar a alguien]
When she screamed "Help!", she scared the daylights out of me.

DEAD

DEAD AS A DOORNAIL
really dead
[verdaderamente muerto]
The cockroach was dead as a doornail after I sprayed it with RoachDed.

DEAD **DUCK***

DEAD **END***

DEAD-END JOB
a job that leads nowhere, that has no future
[un empleo que no da oportunidad de avanzar]
Delivering pizza pies is a dead-end job, say the young men who deliver them.

DROP DEAD
(1) to die suddenly;
[morir de repente]
Mr. Jones dropped dead while playing tennis.

*Look under the **key word*** for this idiom.

_____

(2) an angry expression that is not meant literally
[(como mandato) una expresión de enojo]
I was so angry at him that I told him to drop dead.

_____

KNOCK SOMEONE DEAD

to impress someone; to give an excellent performance or display, and therefore make a superior impression
[impresionarle a alguien]
Julio Iglesias knocked them dead with his singing. He was great.

_____

OVER ONE'S DEAD **BODY***

DEAL

RAW DEAL

bad or unfair treatment
[un tratamiento malo o injusto]
Janice got a raw deal when she bought a car from her neighbor. He never told her that it needed extensive repairs.

_____

DEALER

WHEELER*-DEALER

DEEP

BETWEEN THE DEVIL AND THE DEEP **BLUE*** SEA

GO OFF THE DEEP END

(1) to go into a situation beyond one's ability to handle
[entrar en una situación defícil]
Lee got involved with a married man. She has gone off the deep end.

_____

(2) to get involved in a situation before one is ready.
[envolverse uno en una situacin antes de estar preparado]

Jane went off the deep end by taking a job as a Spanish teacher, though she had studied Spanish for only one term.

_____

DEGREE

THIRD DEGREE

intensive questioning, usually of a person suspected of something
[interrogatorio, generalmente de una persona sospechada de algo]
The police gave Robert the third degree about the robbery. They questioned him for ten hours without letting him rest.

_____

DENT

MAKE A DENT IN

to begin to accomplish something
[comenzar a lograr algo]
I have not made a dent in paying my bills.

_____

DEVIL

BETWEEN THE DEVIL AND THE DEEP **BLUE*** SEA

GIVE THE DEVIL HIS DUE

to give proper credit, even to the enemy
[darle a alguien el reconocimiento debido, hasta al enemigo]
Louie had to admit that Roberto was a superb basketball player, even though they disliked each other. He had to give the devil his due.

_____

DICE

NO DICE

absolutely no
[definitivamente no]
When Dick asked Harry join the social club, he said "No dice."

_____

39

DICK

EVERY TOM, DICK, AND HARRY

everyman; any man; the common man
[cualquier hombre, Fulano]
Every Tom, Dick and Harry in town was invited to the ball.

DIFFERENT

WHISTLE A DIFFERENT TUNE

to change one's story, or to change one's attitude
[cambiar uno sus palabras, o cambiar uno de opinión]
Clara whistled a different tune when she was the driver instead of the complaining passenger.

DILLY-DALLY

DILLY-DALLY

to waste time while doing something
[perder tiempo]
Josie dilly-dallied on the way home from school, and always arrived late.

DIME

DIME A DOZEN

very common, easily available, and inexpensive
[muy común, hallado fácilmente y barato]
Books like this are a dime a dozen.

DIRTY

AIR* ONE'S DIRTY LINEN IN PUBLIC

DIRTY LOOK

scowl; angry look; frown
[mirada de ceño]
She gave me a dirty look when I stepped on her toe by mistake.

DISH

DISH OUT

to give out something in a casual manner, usually food or punishment
[repartir algo, generalmente comidas o castigos]
Amelia was accustomed to being scolded, but she dished out as much as she got.

DO

DO AWAY WITH SOMETHING OR SOMEONE

to eliminate
[eliminar]
The invention of ballpoint pens helped do away with inkbottles.

DO SOMEONE IN

to harm someone
[dañar a alguien]
Manny wanted to win that scholarship, but his low marks in English did him in.

DO (SERVE*) TIME

DOCTOR

DOCTOR UP SOMETHING; DOCTOR SOMETHING UP

to adjust, to fix, to make something look good
[arreglar, ajustar]
Leo doctored up the transmission on the car so that it worked long enough to sell it.

DOG

DOG-TIRED

exhausted
[rendido]
After running the 26 mile marathon, Harry was dog-tired.

*Look under the **key word*** for this idiom.

40

DOGHOUSE

IN THE DOGHOUSE

to be in trouble

[estar metido en líos]

Larry punished Honey for writing with crayons on all the walls in the house; Honey was in the doghouse.

DOGS

RAIN **CATS*** AND DOGS

DOING

NOTHING DOING

absolutely no

[definitivamente no]

When he was asked by the student behind him to cheat on the math test, Joe said "Nothing doing!"

DOLL

DOLL UP; DOLL SOMEONE UP

to dress elegantly, usually for a special occasion, and usually a girl or woman

[vestir a uno o a sí mismo de gala, usualmente una muchacha o una mujer, para una ocasión especial]

The women dolled up for the party, so they were upset to see the men in sneakers and T-shirts.

DOLLAR

$64 DOLLAR **QUESTION***

DOMINO

DOMINO EFFECT

the consequence(s) brought about by one act, which results in another one, and so on, again and again

[las consecuencias producidas por un evento, que luego producen otras, y otras más sucesivamente, como en el derrumbamiento de una fila de dominos parados]

When the Ukraine broke away from the former Soviet Union, this had a domino effect; Uzbekistan, Belorussia and others soon followed.

DONE

EASIER* SAID THAN DONE

DOOR

HAVE ONE'S FOOT IN THE DOOR

to have an early advantage; to have gotten a beginning opening

[tener una ventaja temprana]

Tom has his foot in the door at the nursing home for regular employment because he volunteered there during the summer.

KEEP THE WOLF FROM THE DOOR

to make enough money for the basic necessities, to keep from starving

[ganar dinero suficiente para las necesidades básicas, para salvarse uno del hambre]

Mr. Holmes, on a small salary, supported three children and his wife. He barely kept the wolf from the door.

DOORNAIL

DEAD* AS A DOORNAIL

DOSE

GIVE SOMEONE A DOSE (TASTE) OF HIS/HER OWN MEDICINE

to treat someone in the same manner as he has behaved

[tratar uno a alguien de la misma manera en que éste ha tratado a los demás]

*Look under the **key word*** for this idiom.

*Nellie refused to lend Tom the five dollars he
needed, just as he had done to her. She gave
him a dose of his own medicine.*

DOT

ON THE DOT

exactly on time

[en punto (hora)]

*The train was scheduled to leave at 1:47 PM.
It left on the dot.*

DOUBLE-CHECK

DOUBLE-CHECK

to review twice, very carefully

[revisar dos veces con mucho cuidado]

*I checked and double checked my bank
statement to be sure it was correct.*

DOUBLE-CROSS

DOUBLE-**CROSS***

DOWN

BRING* DOWN THE HOUSE

BUCKLE* DOWN

CLAMP* DOWN

COME* DOWN HARD ON SOMEONE

CRACK* DOWN ON

CUT* SOMEONE DOWN (TO SIZE)

DOWN AND OUT

poor and depressed; defeated, with no hope for
recovery

[en las ultimas; vencido]

*Michael had lost all of his savings, along with
his job. He was down and out.*

DOWN IN THE **DUMPS***

DOWN THE **DRAIN*** (TUBES)

DRESS* DOWN

LOOK* DOWN ON

LOOK* DOWN ONE'S NOSE AT

PUT ONE'S **FOOT*** DOWN

PUT* SOMEONE DOWN

RUN* DOWN

THUMBS* DOWN/UP

TRACK* DOWN

TURN* DOWN

TURN **UPSIDE*** DOWN

WATER* DOWN

WEAR* DOWN

WHEN THE **CHIPS*** ARE DOWN

WIN **HANDS*** DOWN

DOWN-TO-EARTH

DOWN-TO-EARTH

practical

[práctico]

*Sue has good common sense. She is a
down-to-earth person.*

DOZEN

BAKER'S* DOZEN

DIME* A DOZEN

DRABS

IN DRIBS AND DRABS

in little bits; in small instalments

[poco a poco; a plazos pequñeos]

*She paid back the money she owed me in dribs
and drabs. It took a long time.*

DRAG

DRAG OUT SOMETHING; DRAG SOMETHING OUT

to take a longer time than necessary.

[durando un tiempo más largo de lo que es
necesario]

*She dragged out the story by including
unimportant details.*

DRAIN

GO DOWN THE DRAIN (TUBES)

to be lost, wasted

[perderse]

*All their plans for the wedding went down
the drain when Tom lost his job.*

DRAW

BEAT* ONE TO THE DRAW (PUNCH)

DRAW THE LINE

to make a boundary or a limit

[establecer un límite]

When the boys quarrelled, Mom drew the line at their striking each other. That was not allowed.

DRAWING

BACK* TO THE DRAWING BOARD

DRESS

DRESS DOWN SOMEONE

to scold, berate, rebuke

[reñir]

The coach dressed down the team for staying out late the night before the game.

DRESS UP SOMEONE OR SOMETHING; DRESS SOMEONE OR SOMETHING UP

(1) to wear fancy clothing

[vestirse de gala]

Kathy dressed up for the party. She dressed Mary up too.

(2) to make something look better

[mejorar la apariencia]

Joe dressed up the report so that it looked very impressive.

DRIBS

DRIBS AND **DRABS***

DRIVE

DRIVE AT SOMETHING

to aim at, usually in speaking or writing

[apuntar, generalmente por medio de lo hablado o lo escrito]

Paul is not a clear thinker, so it is hard to know what he is driving at.

DRIVE ONE **CRAZY*** (INSANE)

DRIVE SOMEONE UP A **WALL***

DRIVER

BACK*SEAT DRIVER

DROP

DROP BY (IN)

to visit without an appointment

[visitar sin cita previa]

I was surprised and pleased when Nadya dropped by to talk to me.

DROP **DEAD***

DROP IN THE **BUCKET***

DROP OFF SOMEONE OR SOMETHING; DROP SOMEONE OR SOMETHING OFF

to take someone or something to a particular place and leave

[dejar a alguien o algo en un sitio]

Will you drop me off on your way home?

DROPOUT

someone who leaves school or a program before it is completed

[una persona que abandona sus estudios o un programa antes de terminarlos]

Joe was a school dropout and had trouble finding a job.

DROP SOMEONE A LINE; DROP A LINE TO SOMEONE

to write a letter or a postcard

[escribir una carta o una postal a alguien]

When Mrs. Jankow, my teacher, went on vacation, she dropped a line to each of her students.

DROWN

DROWN ONE'S SORROWS

to drink alcoholic beverages because one is unhappy

[beber uno alcohol por no ser feliz]

Tim tried to drown his sorrows with whiskey. It did not help.

DRY

DRY RUN

a practice session

[un ensayo]

He was worried about taking the driving test, and so he asked me to help him do a dry run.

HIGH AND DRY

without help, without support

[sin ayuda o amparo]

Sophie forgot to bring the notes Lucy needed for her lecture. That left Lucy in front of the auditorium, high and dry,

DUCK

A DEAD DUCK

one who has no more opportunities in a situation; one who has failed

[uno desprovisto de oportunidades; un fracasado]

Jules was a dead duck when he came into class without the assignment done.

LAME DUCK

without power, usually referring to an elected official who has not been reelected, but whose term has not yet ended

[sin autoridad, usualmente dicho acerca de un oficial que no ha logrado ser eligido de nuevo, pero cuyo mandato no ha caducado todavía]

After failing to be reelected on Election Day, George Bush became a lame duck president.

QUEER DUCK

a peculiar person

[un tipo raro]

With his baggy pants, unkempt hair and that yellow beret, Antoine is a queer duck.

DUE

GIVE THE **DEVIL*** HIS DUE

DUMPS

TO BE DOWN IN THE DUMPS

to be depressed, dejected

[estar deprimido]

After Sally said she would not marry him, Harry was down in the dumps for a long time.

DUPER

SUPER* DUPER

DUTCH

DUTCH TREAT

the arrangement in which each person pays his share of the cost of a meal or event

[un arreglo en que cada persona paga su propia-parte del costo de una comida o un espectáculo]

The meal was Dutch treat, so the bill was divided equally among the four of us.

GOING DUTCH

SEE **DUTCH*** TREAT

IN DUTCH

in trouble

[en apuros]

She is in Dutch because she did not do her homework.

*Look under the **key word*** for this idiom.

E - F - G

EAGER

EAGER **BEAVER***

EAR

BEND (CHEW) SOMEONE'S EAR

to talk endlessly to someone

[fastidiarle a uno con mucho hablar]

I had a boring lunch with Ruth. She bent my ear talking about her pet cat.

LEND AN EAR

to listen to someone who confides or wants advice

[escucharle a alguien que confía o que pide un consejo]

Dollie is always ready to lend an ear to her friends who have a problem.

PLAY (SOMETHING) BY EAR

(1) to play music after hearing it, but without written notes

[tocar la música de oído]

Many of the famous jazz musicians play by ear.

---

(2) to improvise, responding to the needs of the situation

[actuar de improviso]

Paul tried to anticipate all the questions the interviewer would ask, but in some cases he would have to play it by ear.

PUT A **BUG*** IN ONE'S EAR

EARS

ALL EARS

to be very attentive

[muy atento]

Jane was all ears when they discussed the banquet awards.

UP TO ONE'S EARS IN

overwhelmed; having more than one can manage

[abrumado de]

I'm up to my ears in cartons of books.

WET **BEHIND*** THE EARS

EARTH

DOWN* TO EARTH

SALT* OF THE EARTH

EASE

EASE SOMEONE OUT; EASE OUT SOMEONE

to force someone to leave, but gently

[obligarle a alguien que se retire, pero con suavidad]

The boss eased John out of the position of supervisor by putting him in charge of the stockroom. He also eased out two other supervisors.

ILL AT EASE

to be uncomfortable

[incómodo]

I was ill at ease at the party because I did not know anyone there.

EASIER

EASIER SAID THAN DONE

more difficult than it seems

[más difícil de lo que parece]

Painting that sign is easier said than done.

45

* Look under the **key word*** for this idiom.

EASY

ON EASY STREET
to be comfortably financially
[adinerado]
> The Jones family has been on easy street since they won the lottery.

TAKE IT EASY
to relax; not to work so hard
[descansar; no trabajar tanto]
> Max wears himself out with hard work. He never takes it easy.

EAT

EAT **CROW*** (HUMBLE PIE)
EAT ONE'S **CAKE*** AND HAVE IT TOO
EAT ONE'S **HEART*** OUT
EAT ONE'S WORDS
to admit that what one said was wrong; to retract
[admitir que lo que uno ha dicho fue equivocado]
> Her father said that Deb would not win the art prize. When she did win it, he had to eat his words.

EAT SOMEONE OUT OF HOUSE AND HOME
to eat a lot, and at great cost to someone else
[comer mucho, y a gran costo a otra persona]
> Our growing boys are eating us out of house and home.

EATING

WHAT IS EATING SOMEONE?
What is bothering someone?
[¿Qué le molesta a alguien?]
> Betty has been angry all day. I wonder what is eating her.

EDGE

ON THE EDGE OF ONE'S SEAT
nervous, apprehensive
[nervioso]
> The TV mystery was so exciting it kept me on the edge of my seat.

EFFECT

DOMINO* EFFECT

EGG

BAD* EGG
EGG SOMEONE ON
to urge someone to do something he had not planned to do
[instarle uno a alguien que haga algo que éste no había pensado hacer]
> Moe egged Tim on to climb on the scaffold.

HAVE EGG ON ONE'S FACE
to be embarrassed because of a mistake that is obvious to all
[estar apenado por un error que es obvio a todos]
> Barry had egg on his face when he forgot the name of the person he was introducing as the main speaker.

LAY AN EGG
to fail to live up to expectations
[no cumplir con las espectativas]
> Kate laid an egg when she tried out as a comedienne.

NEST EGG
savings (in cash or in the bank) for a particular purpose
[ahorros (en efectivo o en el banco) destinados a algún propósito especial]
> Ruth has a nest egg for her daughter's college education.

EIGHT-BALL

BEHIND* THE EIGHT-BALL

ELBOW

ELBOW GREASE

energy, hard work

[energía]

*Cleaning the wax off this floor takes a
lot of elbow grease.*

```


```

ELBOW ROOM

a comfortable amount of space

[una cantidad de espacio que es cómoda]

*The teacher asked for a larger classroom for this
group so that there would be more elbow room.*

```


```

ELEPHANT

WHITE ELEPHANT

a valuable possession that is expensive to maintain

[una posesión de mucho valor que es cara de
mantener]

*I will sell my unused and useless wedding presents
at the street fair. They are white elephants.*

```


```

ELEVENTH

ELEVENTH HOUR

the last minute

[al último momento]

*Ron turned in his report to the teacher
at the eleventh hour.*

```


```

END

AT ONE'S WITS' END

not knowing what to do next, desperate

[sin saber cómo continuar, desesperado]

*Ted's parents were at their wits end on
how to help Ted stop drinking,*

```


```

COME* TO THE END OF ONE'S ROPE

A DEAD END

a street that has no exit at one end

[un callejón sin salida]

Avenue X is a dead-end at the railroad tracks.

```


```

DEAD* END JOB

GO OFF THE **DEEP*** END

MAKE ONE'S HAIR STAND ON END

to scare

[espantar]

*When the ghost appeared in the movie, it made
my hair stand on end.*

```


```

PUT AN END TO

to end

[terminar]

*Mom was determined to put an end to
two-hour lunch breaks.*

```


```

GET THE SHORT END OF THE STICK

to get the less desirable portion

[sacar la parte de menos preferencia]

*The supervisor had to decide who would clean
the bathroom; Ellen got the short end of the stick.*

```


```

ENDS

BURN THE CANDLE AT **BOTH*** ENDS

MAKE ENDS MEET

to manage to live on the little money that is available

[lograr vivir con el poco de dinero que le queda a uno]

*Libby is a careful planner. She has always
been able to make ends meet.*

```


```

ODDS AND ENDS

leftover bits of materials

[retazos, desperdicios]

*She used odds and ends of fabric to make
a beautiful patchwork quilt.*

* Look under the **key word*** for this idiom.

EUREKA

EUREKA!

"I have discovered it! I have found the solution."
[¡Eureka!]
> *Eureka! I've been trying to find my lost ring for three years, and I've finally located it.*

EVEN

GET* EVEN WITH

EVEN-STEVEN

EVEN-STEVEN

equal; on the same footing
[en paz]
> *I've paid you the ten dollars I owe you. Now we are even-steven.*

EVERY

HAVE A FINGER IN EVERY PIE

to be involved in everything
[meterse en todo]
> *She's a shrewd businesswoman, and sells many different products. She has a finger in every pie.*

EVERY TOM, **DICK*** AND HARRY

EVIL

GIVE SOMEONE THE EVIL EYE

to put a curse on someone
[maldecir a alguien]
> *Sara said she tripped and fell because Angie had given her the evil eye.*

EYE

APPLE* OF ONE'S EYE
CATCH* ONE'S EYE

GIVE SOMEONE THE **EVIL*** EYE
KEEP AN EYE ON

to watch; observe; take care of
[observar; cuidar]
> *Angelo kept an eye on the pit bulldog to be sure he did not attack anyone.*

SEE EYE TO EYE

to agree
[estar de acuerdo]
> *We see eye to eye on how this house is to be built.*

EYEBROWS

RAISE EYEBROWS

to shock, surprise, dismay people
[chocar, sorprender a los demás]
> *Her miniskirt was so short it raised eyebrows in her workplace.*

EYELASH

BAT* AN EYELASH (NOT TO)

EYES

MAKE EYES AT

to flirt with
[coquetear con]

*Agnes made eyes at one of the boys
that she liked in her class.*

PULL THE WOOL OVER SOMEONE'S EYES
to fool someone
[engañar a alguien]
*That used-car salesman tried to pull the wool
over my eyes by leaving out some of the costs
of leasing the car.*

FACE
FACE THE MUSIC
to accept punishment
[hacer frente al castigo]
*That young man had to face the music for
writing graffiti on the walls of the building.*

FACE UP TO SOMETHING
to accept the truth, or reality, though it may be
unpleasant
[aceptar la verdad por desagradable que sea]
*Andy finally faced up to the fact that smoking
was bad for him, and that he would have to stop.*

HAVE **EGG*** ON ONE'S FACE
MAKE FACES
to grimace, to distort one's face
[hacer muecas]
*When the teacher turned her back, Pat made
faces and the class laughed.*

SAVE FACE
to save one's pride; to avoid humiliation
[evitar la humillación]
*Betsy scorched the main dish, and ruined the
dessert. There was no way she could save
face after that meal.*

TWO-FACED
hypocritical; behaving differently or telling different stories to different people
[hipócrita]
*Tony told Amy he loved her; but he also said
the same thing to Susie. He was two-faced.*

FAIR
FAIR AND SQUARE
even-handed, evenly
[justo]
The teacher divided the prizes fair and square.

FALL
FALL **APART***
LET THE **CHIPS*** FALL WHERE THEY MAY

FALLING
LIKE FALLING OFF A LOG
very easy
[muy fácil]
*For Miriam, making a birthday party for
children was easy. It was like falling off a log.*

FAR
A FAR **CRY*** FROM

FAR-FETCHED
FAR-FETCHED
unlikely, far from the truth
[inverosímil]
*Julie's story of how she rescued the kitten
was far-fetched.*

FAST
FAST **BUCK***
PULL A FAST ONE ON SOMEONE
to trick someone
[engañar a alguien]
*She pulled a fast one on me by not paying for
her meal. She made an excuse and left me
with the check.*

49

FAT

CHEW THE FAT
to chat
[platicar]
Nelson and I love to sit and chew the fat for hours at a time.

FAT **CAT***

FEATHER

BIRDS* OF A FEATHER
A FEATHER IN ONE'S **CAP***
FEATHER ONE'S NEST
to selfishly provide for oneself
[hacer uno su agosto]
It is said that he feathered his nest with the money that was contributed for building a new community center.

FED

FED UP WITH (FED UP TO THE GILLS WITH) SOMEONE OR SOMETHING
tired of
[estar harto con]
I'm fed up with Ted's funny stories.

FEDERAL

MAKE A FEDERAL **CASE*** OUT OF SOMETHING

FEEDS

BITE* THE HAND THAT FEEDS ONE

FEEL

FEEL **BLUE***
FEEL IT IN ONE'S **BONES***
FEEL LIKE TWO **CENTS***
FEEL **LOUSY***

FEET

BACK* ON ONE'S FEET
GET ONE'S FEET WET
to begin something; to do something for the first time

[hacer algo por primera vez]
After practicing dance steps alone, Tom got his feet wet dancing with a girl for the first time at the party.

HAVE COLD FEET
to hold back from doing something because of fear
[dudar uno en hacer algo]
Although Michael could jump into the pool from the side, he has cold feet about diving off the the high board.

HAVE ONE'S FEET ON THE GROUND
to be practical, realistic
[ser práctico]
Miriam has her feet on the ground. She makes good suggestions on how to raise money for the charity,

LAND ON ONE'S FEET
to recover from a difficult situation
[tener éxito después de vivir un tiempo difícil]
After Sol's store burned down, he managed to land on his feet, because he was insured.

NOT TO LET GRASS GROW UNDER ONE'S FEET
to move without delay, do things quickly
[actuar rápidamente]
Dorothy gets every job done quickly. She never lets the grass grow under her feet.

SIX FEET UNDER
dead and buried
[muerto y enterrado]
Ronald wll not get his way about running this company until I'm 6 feet under.

---

* Look under the **key word*** for this idiom.

STAND ON ONE'S OWN TWO FEET
to be independent
[ser independiente]
> *Karl moved from his parents' home when he was 19. He wanted to stand on his own two feet.*

FENCE
SIT ON THE FENCE
to be neutral
[dudar uno en unirse con una u otra facción]
> *The boys were arguing about who was the better soccer player; they asked Ned for his opinion. He refused to say; he preferred to sit on the fence.*

FENDER-BENDER
FENDER-BENDER
a minor automobile accident
[un accidente automovílistico de proporciones menores]
> *Driving out of the parking lot, I hit another car. Fortunately, it was only a fender-bender!*

FETCHED
FAR*-FETCHED

FIDDLE
FIDDLE AROUND
to do something in a haphazard way
[actuar al azar]
> *Joe fiddled around with the tape deck, trying to repair it.*

FIT AS A FIDDLE
in good condition
[de buenas condiciones]
> *Nancy has recovered from her illness. She is now fit as a fiddle.*

PLAY SECOND FIDDLE
to be an assistant; to be in the position next to the top
[hacer uno un papel secundario]
> *Nellie played second fiddle to the director of the play. She worked hard, and he got all the credit.*

FIELD
FROM LEFT FIELD; OUT IN LEFT FIELD
unexpected; unusual, eccentric, inappropriate
[imprevisto; extraño]
> *Zelda seems to be in another world; her suggestions come from left field.*

PLAY* THE FIELD

FIFTH
TAKE THE FIFTH
to refuse to answer questions about oneself that could get one into trouble, as protected by the Fifth Amendment to the U.S. Constitution
[negarse uno a contestar a preguntas sobre sí mismo que podrían meterlo en líos, bajo la protección de la quinta enmendación de la Constitución de los EE.UU.]
> *When asked whether she had been with Ron on the night of the robbery, Sue took the Fifth.*

FIFTY-FIFTY
FIFTY-FIFTY
half and half; not too bad, not too good
[mitad de uno y mitad de otro; más o menos bueno]
> *My chances of winning the race are fifty-fifty.*

FIGHT
FIGHT TOOTH AND NAIL*

FIGURE
BALLPARK* FIGURE

FIGURES

IT FIGURES

That seems to be correct. It makes sense.
[Eso parece correcto (porque conforme con las expectativas).]
It is five miles from home to the library. It figures that it should take at least an hour and a half to walk there.

FILL

FILL THE **BILL***

FILL SOMEONE IN

to give someone information
[enterar a alguien]
I filled Esther in on everything she needed to know for the interview.

FINE-TOOTHED

WITH A FINE-TOOTHED **COMB***

FINGER

HAVE A FINGER IN **EVERY*** PIE

PUT ONE'S FINGER ON

(1) to locate
[ubicar]
I am looking for our January bank statement. Can you put your finger on it?

(2) to identify
[identificar]
I could not quite put my finger on what she is afraid of.

TWIST SOMEONE AROUND ONE'S FINGER

to get someone to do what one wishes; to control someone
[manejar a la gente con maña]
John always does what Dolly wants. She is able to twist him around her little finger.

FINGERS

KEEP ONE'S FINGERS **CROSSED***

HAVE STICKY FINGERS

to have a tendency to steal
[tener la tendencia de robar]
I worry about Judy when we go into a store. She has sticky fingers, and has been arrested twice for shop-lifting.

SLIP THROUGH (SOMEONE'S) FINGERS

to be lost
[perdérselo algo a alguien]
I can't understand why money just slips through my fingers.

FINGERTIPS

HAVE AT ONE'S FINGERTIPS

have readily available in memory or in skill
[saber una cosa al dedillo]
Michael is great at arithmetic; he has the multiplication table at his fingertips.

FIRE

CATCH* FIRE

HAVE MANY IRONS IN THE FIRE

to be doing many things; to be involved in many activities or projects
[interesarse uno por muchas actividades o proyectos]
Lily is always busy because she has so many irons in the fire.

OUT OF THE **FRYING*** PAN INTO THE FIRE

PLAY WITH FIRE

do something dangerous
[hacer algo peligroso]
Riding the bicycle in heavy traffic is playing with fire.

SET FIRE TO SOMETHING
  to burn
  [quemar]
> It is now against the law to set fire to leaves
> or garbage at home.

_____

FIRST
GET TO FIRST **BASE***

FIRSTHAND
FIRSTHAND
  from the original source
  [por si mismo]
> Dan saw that explosion firsthand, while the
> rest of us saw it on TV.

_____

FISH
A FINE KETTLE OF FISH
  a mess
  [un relajo]
> Each of you tells me a different story about
> the accident; this is a fine kettle of fish!

_____

LIKE A FISH OUT OF WATER
  in an unaccustomed place or position
  [fuera de su elemento]
> Fred is uncomfortable wearing a tuxedo;
> he is like a fish out of water.

_____

SMELL SOMETHING FISHY
  to suspect that there is something irregular
  about a situation
  [sospechar]
> Tim says he can't start work on Monday. I smell
> something fishy; I think he has taken another
> job, and will be there that day.

_____

FIST
HAND* OVER FIST

FIT
FIT AS A **FIDDLE***
FIT TO BE TIED
  to be very angry
  [enojadísimo]
> When Sara came late to a supper I had
> made especially for her, I was fit to be tied.

_____

HAVE (THROW) A FIT
  to have an angry outburst, to be angrily excited
  [ponerse uno histérico]
> Mary had a fit when she heard that she could
> not go to camp this summer. She was furious.

_____

FIX
FIX ONE'S WAGON
  to have revenge
  [vengarse uno de alguien]
> Mel fixed Tom's wagon for telling Mom that
> Mel had dirtied up the refrigerator. He hid
> Tom's skates.

_____

FIX SOMEONE UP
  to introduce a young man and a young woman
  [arreglar una cita entre dos personas para que
  se conozcan]
> Mrs. Grant liked Rhona very much, and asked
> her for permission to fix her up with David, a
> very nice young man whom she knew and liked.

_____

FLAME
OLD FLAME
  an old sweetheart
  [un novio antiguo]
> After he returned from the war, Ollie went
> looking for Rosie, his old flame.

_____

* Look under the **key word*** for this idiom.

FLASH

FLASH IN THE PAN

something that happens for a short time only

[algo que perdura solamente por poco tiempo]

Marvin's singing at the show was good but it was a flash in the pan; he never did it again.

FLAT

IN NOTHING FLAT

very quickly; taking very little time

[rapidísimo]

I'll bring back that quart of milk in no time flat.

FLAT AS A PANCAKE

having a smooth, even, level surface

[muy llano o plastado]

The state of Kansas is flat as a pancake; no mountains anywhere.

FLIES

AS THE **CROW*** FLIES

FLIP

FLIP ONE'S LID (FLIP OUT)

to become crazy or very excited

[ponerse loco]

Joel flipped his lid when his two best friends were killed in that automobile accident.

FLOOR

GET IN ON THE GROUND FLOOR

to be part of an activity, program or project at its beginning

[ser participante de una actividad, un programa, o un proyecto en su comienzo]

Donald got in on the ground floor in setting up the local production of ROMEO AND JULIET.

FLY

FLY IN THE OINTMENT

a flaw in an otherwise good thing; something that spoils something else

[lo que estropea algo]

Dan's speech was wonderful. The fly in the ointment was that people in the back of the room could not hear him.

FLY THE **COOP•**

FLY-BY-NIGHT

a temporary, brief, short-lasting business or organization

[un negocio de poca duración]

Many of the dealers at the flea market are fly-by-night operators; they are here one week-end and then you never see them again.

FLY OFF THE HANDLE

to lose one's temper suddenly

[ponerse enfurecido súbitamente]

Mathilda flew off the handle when Riccardo asked her how old she is.

GO FLY A KITE!

Go away! Don't bother me!

[¡Lárgate;! ¡Lárgue (n) se!]

Jaime told Rosalie to go fly a kite when she said she wanted to go to the movies with him

FLYING

COME THROUGH (PASS) WITH FLYING **COLORS***

FOLLOW

FOLLOW ONE'S NOSE

to continue in the direction in which one is going

[ir recto]

When Joe asked where to find the Corn Flakes in the supermarket, the cashier told him to go to Aisle 3 and follow his nose.

FOOL

FOOL AROUND, MESS AROUND, HORSE AROUND
to act childishly
[hacerse el niño]
The college students fooled around in the kitchen until they broke the table.

_____

NOBODY'S FOOL
somebody smart
[alguien inteligente]
Ivan is modest, but he is nobody's fool.

_____

FOOT

FOOT THE BILL*
GET OFF (START OFF) ON THE WRONG FOOT
to make a mistake at the very beginning
[cometer un error en el comienzo]
On her first day on the job, Mary wore jeans and chewed gum. She started off on the wrong foot.

_____

HAVE ONE'S FOOT IN THE DOOR*
PUT ONE'S FOOT DOWN
to insist
[insistir]
The teacher put her foot down. She wanted no gum-chewing in her classroom.

_____

PUT ONE'S FOOT IN ONE'S MOUTH
to say the wrong thing; to say something embarrassing
[decir una cosa indiscreta]
When she asked how I liked the green outfit she was wearing, I put my foot in my mouth by saying that I do not like the color green.

_____

FORKED

SPEAK WITH FORKED TONGUE
to be a hypocrite; to lie

[ser hipócrita]
Jamie told me he likes Louisa but he told Maria that he hates her. He speaks with a forked tongue.

_____

FORTY

FORTY WINKS
a short nap
[una siesta]
After that exhausting hike, I lay down for forty winks. I needed the rest.

_____

FOUL

MESS (LOUSE, FOUL) UP SOMETHING; MESS SOMETHING UP
to ruin something
[estropear algo]
She fouled up (messed up) the cake I was baking by insisting on putting in twice as much flour as the recipe called for.

_____

FREAK

FREAK OUT
to lose one's composure
[emocionarse mucho]
The teacher asked me to write my spelling words 300 times each. After 100 times, I freaked out.

_____

FREE

FREE-FOR-ALL
a commotion in which everyone shoves, makes noise, and sometimes hits
[una conmoción en que la gente empuja, grita y a veces golpea]
A free-for-all broke out when Pedro hit Rafael in the schoolyard and other boys joined in the pushing and shoving.

_____

SCOT-FREE
completely free, without restraint

* Look under the **key word*** for this idiom.

[sin castigo]
After the trial, Desmond was declared innocent and went home scot-free.

FREEZES
TILL **HELL** * FREEZES OVER

FRIEND
BOSOM * FRIEND

FRINGE
FRINGE **BENEFITS** *

FRITZ
ON THE FRITZ
to be broken, not working
[descompuesto]
My weekend is ruined because my car is on the fritz. It won't run.

FRONT
FRONT FOR
to be secretly in the service of
[servir algo como pretexto para]
The laundromat was a front for a drug operation.

PUT UP A GOOD FRONT
to act as though things were going well, even when they are not
[hacer de tripas corazón]
Though her report card was bad, Cindy did not show her disappointment. She put up a good front with her classmates.

UP FRONT
in advance
[de antemano]
The salesman wanted $200 up front if we wanted to buy the car.

FRYING
OUT OF THE FRYING PAN INTO THE FIRE
to go from a bad situation to one that is worse
[huir del fuego y dar en las brasas]
Emma went out of the frying pan into the fire when she quit her job at the factory around the corner from her home and had to take the same job that paid less and was miles away.

FULL
FULL **HOUSE** *
HAVE ONE'S HANDS FULL
to have too many things to do
[tener demasiado para hacer]
Tina could not accept any more tasks to do; she has her hands full right now taking care of her sick mother and the baby.

SHOOT FULL OF **HOLES** *

FUSE
BLOW * A FUSE

FUSS
KICK UP A FUSS
to complain loudly
[quejarse uno a voces]
Josie kicked up a big fuss about the scratch Tony gave her.

GAIN
NO PAIN, NO GAIN.
In order to make progress, one must pay a price.
[Para avanzar, hay que pagar un precio.]
After I broke my leg, the exercises hurt me a lot. When I complained, the doctor said, "No pain, no gain."

GANDER
TAKE A GANDER AT SOMETHING
to look at something
[echar una mirada a]
Take a gander at her jewelry. It is so beautiful.

GAS

STEP* ON THE GAS (STEP ON IT)

GASKET

BLOW* A GASKET

GET

GET A CHARGE (**BANG***) OUT OF

GET A GRIP ON ONESELF

to control one's feelings

[controlar uno sus emociones]

Randy was very angry at Sarah, but she got a grip on herself and calmed down before the meeting.

GET A HANDLE ON SOMETHING

to understand something

[comprender]

I finally got a handle on Cubist art. I am beginning to understand it, although I still do not like it.

GET A KICK (**BANG***, CHARGE) OUT OF

GET A LIFE! (NOTE: NO VARIATION!).

Act sensibly! Choose good goals in life!

[No seas tonto! No sea(n) tonto(s)!]

Stop borrowing money from your friends. Get a job and get a life.

GET A MOVE ON

to hurry

[darse prisa]

Danny is so slow. If he doesn't get a move on, we're going to miss that train.

GET A RISE OUT OF SOMEONE

to get an angry or irritated reaction

[enojar a (alguien)]

Tony is trying hard to get a rise out of Alice, but she is paying no attention.

GET A TASTE (**DOSE***) OF ONE'S MEDICINE

GET AWAY WITH MURDER

to go unpunished or pay a small price for something

[sacar un castigo leve o ninguno]

Seth broke all the dishes, but was not punished. His mother is so fond of him that she lets him get away with murder.

GET **BURNED***

GET **CARRIED*** AWAY

GET DOWN TO **BRASS*** TACKS

GET EVEN WITH SOMEONE

to get revenge on someone

[vengarse de]

Sharon got even with Kent for losing her math book. She spilled ink on his lab notebook.

GET (BE) HELD UP

(1) to be accosted by a robber

[ser robado]

Florence got held up last night just after she left the bank teller machine.

(2) to be delayed

[ser demorado]

Though he left on time, Nat got held up because the subway ran behind schedule, and so he was late.

GET HOT UNDER THE **COLLAR***

GET IN ON THE GROUND **FLOOR***

GET IN SOMEONE'S HAIR

to annoy someone

[molestar a alguien]

His little sister got in Barney's hair when he was trying to study for his final exams.

_____

GET INTO THE SWING OF THINGS
   to become comfortable in a new environment
   [acostumbrarse uno de un nuevo ambiente]
   It took Charlie one whole semester to get into the swing of things when he went off to college.

_____

GET IN TOUCH* WITH
GET IT
   to understand
   [comprender]
   The first time the teacher explained how to do long division, Andy didn't get it.

_____

GET IT OFF ONE'S CHEST*
GET LOST! (NOTE: NO VARIATION!)
   Leave! Go away!
   [Largate!; Largue(n)se!]
   The boys did not want Tim with them on their bicycle trip. They told him to get lost.

_____

GET OFF IT! (NOTE: NO VARIATION!)
   Stop pretending!
   [¡No te hagas! ¡No se haga(n)!]
   Thelma, you're not an actress, so get off it, and take some lessons.

_____

GET OFF ON THE WRONG FOOT*
GET OFF SOMEONE'S BACK*
GET OFF THE GROUND
   to make a good start
   [empezar bien]
   I just found a new apartment. My plans to move have finally gotten off the ground.

_____

GET ON SOMEONE'S NERVES
   to irritate someone
   [molestar a alguien]
   The noise of the refrigerator motor gets on Ben's nerves.

_____

GET (CLIMB, JUMP) ON THE BANDWAGON*
GET ONE'S FEET* WET
GET SOMEONE'S GOAT
   to anger (someone)
   [enojar a (alguien)]
   He gets my goat every time he coughs into people's faces.

_____

GET ONE'S OWN WAY
   to do as one wishes
   [hacer uno lo que se le antoje]
   Reva preferred to have her bread toasted. and she got her own way.

_____

GET OUT FROM UNDER
   to overcome a difficult, wearing and frustrating problem
   [salir uno bien después de un contratiempo]
   Jose finally got out from under when his sister agreed to taking care of their elderly mother.

_____

GET OUT OF HAND
   to become difficult to control
   [ponerse uno difícil de controlar]
   Timmy is a restless child. He quickly gets out of hand.

_____

GET OUT OF LINE
   to take a rebellious position
   [actuar de una manera refractaria]
   Caroline ignored the dress code in her school. She was punished because she got out of line.

GET OVER
to recover
[recuperarse uno la salud; vencer]
It did not take me long to get over the flu.

GET SMART
be sensible
[se inteligente]
Alex told his friend Gene to get smart and stop smoking.

GET SOMETHING OFF ONE'S **CHEST***
GET STEAMED UP
to become angry
[enojarse]
I got steamed up when she teased me about my boyfriend.

GET TAKEN
to be taken advantage of
[ser engañado]
Ronald got taken by the salesman who persuaded him to buy a defective stereo..

GET THE **AXE***
GET THE **BETTER*** OF
GET THE **BRUSH*** OFF
GET THE **COLD*** SHOULDER
GET THE RUNAROUND
to be misdirected, or given false information
[recibir información falsa]
Instead of telling me exactly where to get the application for the city job, they gave me the runaround.

GET THE SHORT **END*** OF THE STICK
GET THE UPPER HAND
to overpower, to take control
[dominar]
As they wrestled, Olaf pinned his opponent to the floor, got the upper hand, and won.

GET THROUGH TO SOMEONE
to communicate with someone despite difficulties
[comunicarse uno con (alguien) a pesar de las dificultades]
I can't seem to get through to you; you don't hear anything that I say.

GET TO FIRST **BASE***
GET TO THE **BOTTOM*** OF (SOMETHING)
GET UNDER SOMEONE'S SKIN
to annoy, to irritate
[fastidiar]
Darryl gets under Foster's skin with her constant nagging.

GET UP ON THE WRONG SIDE OF THE **BED***
GET WIND OF
to hear about
[oír noticias de]
Lulu got wind of the news that the principal might retire at the end of the year.

GET WITH IT
to be aware, and to act accordingly
[enterarse y actuar según lo sabido]
Morty was usually quite absent-minded. When he drove the car, his wife reminded him to get with it and pay attention to the road signs.

LET'S GET THE SHOW ON THE ROAD (NOTE: NO VARIATION!)
Let's start the project!

* Look under the **key word*** for this idiom.

[¡Comencemos el proyecto!]
Eager for the project to start, Sandra said,
"Let's get the show on the road!"

_____

GETTER

GO*-GETTER

GHOST

NOT TO HAVE A GHOST OF A CHANCE*

GIFT

DON'T LOOK A GIFT HORSE IN THE MOUTH!
(NOTE: USUALLY IN THE PRESENT TENSE)

Do not criticize a gift or something good that
has happened!

[¡No critique(n)(s) un regalo o lo bueno que ha
pasado!]

John's parents bought him a used bicycle. He
complained about it, so they took it back. Now
he has nothing. He should not have looked a gift
horse in the mouth.

_____

GILLS

FED* UP TO THE GILLS WITH

GIVE

GIVE IN

to yield

[rendirse]

Saul gave in when he saw that Tom had proof
that he was right.

_____

GIVE IT ONE'S BEST* SHOT

GIVE IT TO SOMEONE STRAIGHT

to tell the truth

[decir la verdad]

Charles gave it to Martin straight: he would
need six months to finish the assignment.

_____

GIVE SOMEONE A BIG* HAND

GIVE SOMEONE A BREAK*

GIVE SOMEONE A DOSE* (TASTE) OF HIS OWN MEDICINE

GIVE SOMEONE A HARD TIME, GIVE A HARD TIME TO SOMEONE

to make things difficult for someone

[darle a alguien dificultades]

Jimmy gave me a hard time when I took care
of him as a baby-sitter. He was up all night.

_____

GIVE SOMEONE A PAIN; GIVE A PAIN TO SOMEONE

to irritate someone

[molestar a alguien]

Walter gives me a pain every time he visits.
He complains about everything.

_____

GIVE SOMEONE A PIECE OF ONE'S MIND; GIVE A PIECE OF
ONE'S MIND TO SOMEONE

to scold someone

[reñir a alguien]

Andrew's paint job is bad, and I told him so.
I was angry and I gave him a piece of my mind.

_____

GIVE SOMEONE A SNOW JOB; GIVE A SNOW JOB TO
SOMEONE

to deceive or confuse someone

[decepciónar o confundir a alguien]

The used-car salesman told me his cars were
well cared for. I knew it was a snow job because
I saw the rust and small dents on the bodywork.

_____

GIVE SOMEONE A TONGUE LASHING; GIVE A TONGUE
LASHING TO SOMEONE

to scold someone

[regañar a alguien]

When Kel tripped me and hurt my ankle, I was
furious and gave him a tongue lashing.

_____

GIVE SOMEONE HIS OR HER WALKING PAPERS; GIVE
WALKING PAPERS TO SOMEONE

to fire or let go from a position

[despedirle a alguien de su empleo]

Sam gave the bookkeeper her walking papers
because she was insolent.

GIVE SOMEONE THE **EVIL*** EYE

GIVE SOMEONE (**GET***) THE RUNAROUND

GIVE THE **BRUSH***-OFF

GIVE THE **COLD*** SHOULDER

GIVE THE DEVIL HIS **DUE***

GLOVES

HANDLE WITH KID GLOVES

to be very gentle and careful in dealing with someone or something

[ser muy amable y cuidados con una persona, una situación o una cosa]

> *She is very sensitive, and must be handled with kid gloves.*

GO

GO AGAINST THE **GRAIN***

GO **BANANAS***

GO **DUTCH***

GO **FLY*** A KITE

GO-GETTER

one who works hard and is effective and enthusiastic

[uno quien trabaja duro y es efectivo y entusiástico]

> *Nancy is a go-getter in selling household supplies.*

GO INTO A **HUDDLE***

GO OFF THE **DEEP*** END

GO STEADY

to have an exclusive ongoing relationship, usually with someone of the opposite sex

[ser novios un hombre y una mujer]

> *Tom and Mary have been going steady for three years. They spend time together several times a week and will be married this month.*

GO STRAIGHT

to become law-abiding

[terminar por obedecer a la ley]

> *After he got out of jail, Terry decided to go straight, and get a steady job.*

GO THROUGH **CHANNELS***

GO TO **BAT*** FOR

GO TO PIECES

to become unable to function

[hacerse uno incapaz de funcionar]

> *Jack is very sensitive. If it were not for the help of his aunt, Jack would have gone to pieces years ago.*

GO TO POT

to be ruined

[arruinarse]

> *That beautiful building will go to pot if it is not occupied and taken care of.*

GO TO TOWN

(1) to be extravagant

[ser extravagante con el dinero]

> *Lulu really went to town for Mort's fiftieth birthday party. They dined at the Ritz.*

(2) to work hard and quickly

[trabajar duro y de prisa]

> *Stan went to town on that construction job. He finished it in two weeks.*

GO UNDER THE KNIFE

to have surgery, to be operated on

[sufrir una operación]

> *Joe went under the knife for appendicitis this morning.*

GO UP IN SMOKE

to disappear, to be wasted

[desaparecer]

61

Larry is a spendthrift. His inheritance went up in smoke.

_____

GO WITHOUT SAYING
to be obvious
[estar algo comprendido; sin necesidad de palabras]
It goes without saying that Lou and Irene are a devoted couple. They are always holding hands.

_____

MAKE* A GO OF
TOUCH* AND GO

GOAT
GET ONE'S **GOAT***

GOING
HAVE SOMETHING GOING FOR ONE
to have an advantage
[tener la ventaja]
Ellen has something going for her. She is charming.

_____

KNOW IF ONE IS **coming*** OR GOING

GOLD
GOLD MINE
a great opportunity for earning money
[una gran oportunidad para ganar dinero]
The neighborhood video rental shops are very successful; they are a gold mine for their owners.

_____

GOOD
FOR GOOD
forever
[para siempre]
It is too bad that Tony quit school for good.

_____

GOOD SPORT
one who accepts defeat or disappointment gracefully
[buen perdedor]
Sissy was a good sport about giving up her birthday party. She said it would be better next year.

_____

KEEP GOOD TIME
(for a watch or clock) to be accurate
[marchar un reloj bien]
My old watch kept good time; my new one does not.

_____

MAKE GOOD TIME
to travel more quickly than expected
[viajar más rápido de lo que se esperaba]
We made good time driving from New York to Boston; it took us only four hours.

_____

PUT UP A GOOD **FRONT***

GOODBYE
KISS SOMETHING GOODBYE
to expect never to see something again
[esperar uno no volver a ver alguna cosa]
When you lend a book to Kathy, you can kiss it goodbye. You will never get it back.

_____

GOODS
SELL SOMEONE A **BILL*** OF GOODS

GOOF
GOOF OFF
to avoid work,
[holgar]
Tanya goofed off while the rest of us prepared the meal.

_____

GOOF-OFF

a lazy person
[una persona perezosa]
Tanya is a goof off. She does not do her work.

_____

GOOSE

A WILD GOOSE **CHASE***
COOK* SOMEONE'S GOOSE

GRABS

UP FOR GRABS

not reserved; to be available to whoever
comes first and chooses
[no reservada, libre]
*At the end of the birthday party, the colorful
balloons were up for grabs.*

_____

GRAIN

AGAINST THE GRAIN

against one's natural inclinations
[a contrapelo]
*It goes against the grain for me to profit from
someone's sickness.*

_____

TAKE WITH A GRAIN OF SALT

to doubt a statement; not to believe something
completely
[dudar uno una declaración]
*I took the report of Len's high salary with a
grain of salt. Len is known to exaggerate.*

_____

GRANTED

TAKE SOMETHING FOR GRANTED

to accept something as true, without question
[dar por supuesto]
*Mary took it for granted that the children would
go on vacation with her and her husband.*

_____

GRAPES

SOUR GRAPES

pretense that a disappointment is not important
or worthwhile
[fingir no estar desilusionado después de perder
una oportunidad]
*Van missed the chance to buy Goody's car;
then he said he didn't want it anyway because
it had many defects. It was sour grapes on his part.*

_____

GRAPEVINE

THROUGH THE GRAPEVINE

by rumor
[por medio de rumor]
*We heard about the holiday party through
the grapevine.*

_____

GRASS

NOT TO LET GRASS GROW UNDER ONE'S **FEET***

GRAVY

BE ON THE GRAVY TRAIN

to be rich
[ser rico]
*Since he got that job in the stock market,
he has been on the gravy train.*

_____

GREASE

ELBOW* GREASE
GREASE MONKEY

a mechanic by trade
[un mecánico]
*Tommy is a grease monkey. He will repair the
muffler in my car.*

_____

GREASY

GREASY SPOON

cheap restaurant, with mainly fatty food
[restaurante de nivel bajo, principalmente de
comidas grasosas]
*Paul stopped at the greasy spoon for his usual
french fried potatoes and a hamburger.*

* Look under the **key word*** for this idiom.

GRIN

GRIN LIKE A CHESHIRE **CAT***

GRIND

AN **AXE*** TO GRIND

GRINDSTONE

KEEP ONE'S NOSE TO THE GRINDSTONE

to work without stopping

[continuar trabajando siempre]

Lily keeps her nose to the grindstone. She never rests.

GRIP

GET* A GRIP ON ONESELF

GRIPE

BELLYACHE (**BEEF***, GRIPE, KICK, SQUAWK))

GROUND

COVER* A LOT OF GROUND

GET IN ON THE GROUND **FLOOR***

GET* OFF THE GROUND

HAVE ONE'S **FEET*** ON THE GROUND

ON SHAKY GROUND

not well founded

[en una situación dudosa]

He is on shaky ground when he applies for a senior discount card, because he is only 58.

GROW

NOT TO LET GRASS GROW UNDER ONE'S **FEET***

GUESS

TO SECOND GUESS

to give an opinion after a previous action has been shown to be wrong

[ofrecer una segunda opinión después de ver rechazada la primera]

After John asked for a raise in pay and was turned down, Sally second guessed that he should not have asked for the raise.

GUN

JUMP THE GUN

to start doing something before the proper time

[empezar a hacer algo antes de la hora indicada]

Leon jumped the gun in selling his paintings before the art appraiser had evaluated them.

GUNS

STICK TO ONE'S GUNS

to be firm in defending one's belief or action

[quedarse uno firme en defensa de sus creencias o acciones]

I stuck to my guns; I supported the candidates who voted for civil rights.

H - I - J - K

HABIT

KICK A HABIT

to change a fixed pattern of harmful behavior

[dejar un hábito nocivo]

It was very hard for Sharon to kick the habit of smoking.

HAIR

MAKE ONE'S HAIR STAND ON **END***

GET IN SOMEONE'S **HAIR***

LET* ONE'S HAIR DOWN

HAIRS

SPLIT HAIRS

to make petty distinctions; to quibble

[ser quisquilloso]

I estimated that the curtains would cost about 25 dollars. Sue said they would cost 26 dollars. Sue tends to split hairs when discussing costs.

HALF-BAKED

HALF-**BAKED***

HALFHEARTED

HALFHEARTED

without enthusiasm

[sin entusiasmo]

She accepted the invitation to the ball half-heartedly, because she was Sam's second choice.

HALFWAY

MEET ONE HALFWAY

to compromise

[hacer concesiones a una persona]

I wanted to leave at 3; Mona wanted to leave at 2. She met me halfway: we left at 2:30.

HANCOCK

JOHN HANCOCK

one's signature

[la firma de alguien]

All that was left to do was to sign the lease. So we put our John Hancocks on it, and now we have a fine apartment.

HAND

BITE* THE HAND THAT FEEDS ONE

GET* OUT OF HAND

GET* THE UPPER HAND

GIVE SOMEONE A **BIG*** HAND

HAND IT TO SOMEONE

to give someone credit

[atribuirle a alguien el mérito]

I must hand it to Helen. She had knee surgery yesterday, and today she is back on the job.

HAND OVER **FIST***

HAND TO MOUTH

barely able to cover expenses

[vivir al día]

Many of the unemployed are living hand to mouth.

HAVE ONE'S HAND IN THE TILL

to steal from an organization

[estar con las manos en la masa]

When the boss checked the cash register receipts, she found that some money was missing. Someone's hands were in the till.

OLD HAND

an experienced person

[una persona experimentada]

Aaron is an old hand with horses; he will take good care of that animal.

*Look under the **key word*** for this idiom.

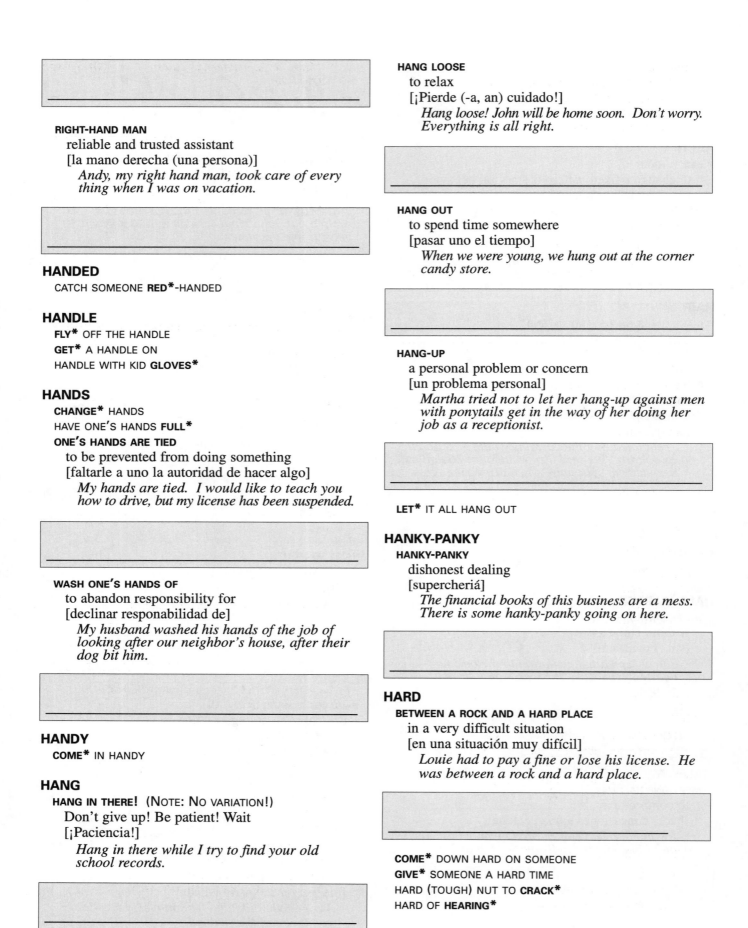

RIGHT-HAND MAN
    reliable and trusted assistant
    [la mano derecha (una persona)]
        Andy, my right hand man, took care of every thing when I was on vacation.

HANDED
CATCH SOMEONE **RED***-HANDED

HANDLE
FLY* OFF THE HANDLE
GET* A HANDLE ON
HANDLE WITH KID **GLOVES***

HANDS
CHANGE* HANDS
HAVE ONE'S HANDS **FULL***
ONE'S HANDS ARE TIED
    to be prevented from doing something
    [faltarle a uno la autoridad de hacer algo]
        My hands are tied. I would like to teach you how to drive, but my license has been suspended.

WASH ONE'S HANDS OF
    to abandon responsibility for
    [declinar responabilidad de]
        My husband washed his hands of the job of looking after our neighbor's house, after their dog bit him.

HANDY
COME* IN HANDY

HANG
HANG IN THERE! (NOTE: NO VARIATION!)
    Don't give up! Be patient! Wait
    [¡Paciencia!]
        Hang in there while I try to find your old school records.

HANG LOOSE
    to relax
    [¡Pierde (-a, an) cuidado!]
        Hang loose! John will be home soon. Don't worry. Everything is all right.

HANG OUT
    to spend time somewhere
    [pasar uno el tiempo]
        When we were young, we hung out at the corner candy store.

HANG-UP
    a personal problem or concern
    [un problema personal]
        Martha tried not to let her hang-up against men with ponytails get in the way of her doing her job as a receptionist.

LET* IT ALL HANG OUT

HANKY-PANKY
HANKY-PANKY
    dishonest dealing
    [supercheriá]
        The financial books of this business are a mess. There is some hanky-panky going on here.

HARD
BETWEEN A ROCK AND A HARD PLACE
    in a very difficult situation
    [en una situación muy difícil]
        Louie had to pay a fine or lose his license. He was between a rock and a hard place.

COME* DOWN HARD ON SOMEONE
GIVE* SOMEONE A HARD TIME
HARD (TOUGH) NUT TO **CRACK***
HARD OF **HEARING***

*Look under the **key word*** for this idiom.   **66**

HARD UP
  desperately needing money
  [apurado de dinero]
  *We're hard up this year and can't afford
  expensive holiday gifts.*

HARP
  HARP ON
  to keep talking about one subject
  [repetir constantemente]
  *She harps on her need for exercise, but she
  does not leave time for doing it.*

HARRY
  EVERY TOM, **DICK*** AND HARRY

HAS-BEEN
  HAS-BEEN
  a person whose fame and popularity have declined
  [una vieja gloria]
  *Some people say Gorbachev is a has-been.
  Only time will tell.*

HASH
  SLING HASH
  to be a waiter or a waitress
  [ser camarero(-a)]
  Mollie slings hash at the local diner.

HAT
  KEEP SOMETHING UNDER ONE'S HAT
  to keep something secret
  [guardar algo en secreto]
  *Michelle told no one about the special event.
  She kept it under her hat.*

  OLD HAT
  out of style; not new
  [anticuado]

*Using a typewriter instead of a word processor
is old hat.*

TAKE ONE'S HAT OFF TO SOMEONE
  to admire someone
  [admirar a alguien]
  I take my hat off to Michael for stopping smoking.

TALK* THROUGH ONE'S HAT

HATCHED
  COUNT ONE'S **CHICKENS*** BEFORE THEY ARE HATCHED

HATCHET
  BURY* THE HATCHET

HAUL
  HAUL (RAKE) OVER THE **COALS***

HAVE
  HAVE A **BALL***
  HAVE A **BLAST***
  HAVE A **CHIP*** ON ONE'S SHOULDER
  HAVE A **CRUSH*** ON
  HAVE (THROW) A **FIT***
  HAVE A FINGER IN **EVERY*** PIE
  HAVE A GO AT SOMETHING
  to try something
  [tratar de hacer algo]
  I'll have a go at opening that jar.

  HAVE A GOOD **HEAD*** ON ONE'S SHOULDERS
  HAVE A LOT ON THE **BALL***
  HAVE A **MIND*** OF ONE'S OWN
  HAVE A **SCREW*** LOOSE
  HAVE A **VOICE*** IN
  HAVE ANOTHER **GUESS*** (THINK) COMING
  HAVE AT ONE'S **FINGERTIPS***
  HAVE **CONNIPTIONS***
  HAVE **EGG*** ON ONE'S FACE
  HAVE MANY IRONS IN THE **FIRE***
  HAVE IT **COMING***
  HAVE IT IN FOR SOMEONE
  to have a bad feeling about someone and plan
  to cause that person pain or trouble
  [guardarle rencor a alguien]

*Look under the **key word*** for this idiom.

Ted has it in for Gil for wrecking his car. Ted is trying to make Gil lose his job.

_____

HAVE IT MADE*

HAVE IT OUT WITH SOMEONE
to argue with someone about a personal disagreement
[discutir algo con alguien]
Margaret has been making false accusations against me. I'm going to have it out with her.

_____

HAVE ONE'S **BACK*** TO THE WALL
HAVE ONE'S **CAKE*** AND EAT IT TOO
HAVE ONE'S **FEET*** ON THE GROUND
HAVE ONE'S FOOT IN THE **DOOR***
HAVE ONE'S **HAND*** IN THE TILL
HAVE ONE'S HANDS **FULL***
HAVE ONE'S **HEART*** SET ON
HAVE ONE'S HEAD IN THE **CLOUDS***
HAVE ONE'S **WAY***
HAVE PULL (**CLOUT***, AN IN)
HAVE SOMEONE'S **NUMBER***
HAVE SOMETHING **GOING*** FOR ONE
HAVE SOMETHING UP ONE'S **SLEEVE***
HAVE STICKY **FINGERS***
HAVE THE **JITTERS***
HAVE TWO **STRIKES*** AGAINST ONE
HAVE WHAT IT **TAKES***
NOT TO HAVE A **LEG*** TO STAND ON

HAY

HIT THE HAY (SACK)
to go to bed
[acostarse]
It was past 9 o'clock and time for the children to hit the hay.

_____

HEAD

BITE* ONE'S HEAD OFF

HAVE A GOOD HEAD ON ONE'S SHOULDERS
to be sensible
[ser práctico]
Henry is very practical. He has a good head on his shoulders.

_____

HAVE ONE'S HEAD IN THE **CLOUDS***

HEAD OVER HEELS IN LOVE
totally in love
[completamente enamorado]
They are head over heels in love.

_____

HIT THE NAIL ON THE HEAD
to be correct
[tener razón]
Elsie hit the nail on the head when she gave the right answer to the question.

_____

HOTHEAD
a person who loses his/her temper easily
[enojón]
I try to keep calm with Delia. She is such a hothead.

_____

KEEP ONE'S HEAD
to stay calm in an emergency
[mantenerse uno tranquilo en una emergencia]
Mel kept his head when his car went out of control. He managed to stop safely.

_____

KEEP ONE'S HEAD ABOVE WATER
to be able to manage on one's funds
[poder vivir del dinero que uno tiene]
When I lost my job, we managed to keep our heads above water with our savings until I found a new job.

_____

KNOCK* ONE'S HEAD AGAINST THE WALL

LOSE ONE'S HEAD (NOODLE)
to become confused, irrational, to panic
[ponerse confundido o irracional]
There is no need to lose your head because of what Phil said. Phil is a liar.

_____

*Look under the **key word*** for this idiom.

OFF THE TOP OF ONE'S HEAD

spontaneously, without careful thought

[de improviso]

> *Ted did not prepare for the oral examination. He answered the questions off the top of his head.*

OUT OF ONE'S HEAD

insane

[loco]

> *I must have been out of my head to take on this enormous responsibility.*

PUT SOMETHING OUT OF ONE'S HEAD (MIND)

to forget something purposely

[olvidar algo de adrede]

> *I want to write a family history, but I put it out of my head because I am so busy.*

HEADS

PUT OUR (YOUR, THEIR) HEADS TOGETHER

to confer

[conferir]

> *This is a difficult problem. Let's put our heads together to plan the engagement party.*

HEALTH

CLEAN **BILL*** OF HEALTH

HEARING

HARD OF HEARING

partially or totally deaf

[duro de oído]

> *Speak louder. Tony is hard of hearing.*

HEART

EAT ONE'S HEART OUT

to be envious or sad

[estar envidioso o triste]

> *I ate my heart out because I could not go to the wedding.*

HAVE ONE'S HEART SET ON SOMETHING

to want something very much

[desear algo mucho]

> *He had his heart set on buying that ten-speed bicycle.*

HEART-TO-HEART

intimate and frank

[íntimo y franco]

> *Frank and his father had a heart-to-heart talk about drugs and drinking.*

LEARN SOMETHING BY HEART

to memorize

[aprender de memoria]

> *The teacher wanted us to learn the Declaration of Independence by heart.*

ONE'S HEART IS IN ONE'S MOUTH

to be nervous, fearful

[estar nervioso]

> *My heart was in my mouth when Martin drove on the narrow roads in the mountains.*

ONE'S HEART IS IN THE RIGHT PLACE

to have good intentions

[tener buenas intenciones]

> *Mollie gave us a sweater that was too small for the baby, but her heart was in the right place.*

ONE'S HEART IS NOT IN IT

One is unenthusiastic.

[Alguien no está entusiástico]

Myra's heart is not in this project.
She is often absent from meetings.

_____

TAKE SOMETHING TO HEART
to consider something seriously
[tomar algo a pecho]
> *Libby took to heart the criticisms of her*
> *appearance and is changing her wardrobe.*

_____

HEAT
PUT THE HEAT (SCREWS) ON
to put pressure on
[presionar]
> *The police put the heat on the street vendors*
> *and made them disperse.*

_____

HEAVEN
IN SEVENTH HEAVEN
very happy
[muy contento]
> *Jane has been in seventh heaven since her*
> *engagement to Robert.*

_____

HEELED
WELL*-HEELED

HEELS
HEAD* OVER HEELS

HELD
GET* (BE) HELD UP

HELL
SNOWBALL'S CHANCE* IN HELL
COME* HELL OR HIGH WATER
TILL HELL FREEZES OVER
forever
[para siempre]
> *I will keep this book till Hell freezes over.*

_____

HERE
THE BUCK* STOPS HERE.

HIGH
COME* HELL OR HIGH WATER
HIGH AND DRY*
LIVE HIGH OFF THE HOG
to live extravagantly, luxuriously
[vivir de lujo]
> *The Smiths live high off the hog. Their home is*
> *spectacular and they drive a new Mercedes.*

_____

ON ONE'S HIGH HORSE*

HILT
TO THE HILT
to the limit, to the maximum
[hasta el límite]
> *Jason defended his brother to the hilt.*

_____

HIP
SHOOT FROM THE HIP
to react quickly and directly
[reaccionar rápidamente]
> *Muriel is a poor trial lawyer. She often loses*
> *arguments because she shoots from the hip.*

_____

HIT
HIT BELOW THE BELT*
HIT IT OFF
to like someone
[hacer buenas migas con]
> *We hit it off the first time we met, and have*
> *become good friends since then.*

_____

HIT SOMEONE UP FOR SOMETHING
to ask someone for something
[pedirle algo a alguien]
> *Joan needed some money so she hit Jack up*
> *for a loan.*

_____

HIT THE **BOTTLE***

HIT THE **CEILING*** (ROOF)

HIT THE **HAY*** (SACK)

HIT THE NAIL ON THE **HEAD***

HIT THE ROAD

to leave, to begin a trip

[irse]

> Marvin hit the road early so that he could get to Chicago by the end of the day.

_____

HIT THE SKIDS

to be worthless, economically

[empeorarse económicamente]

> During the Depression, unemployment rose and many people hit the skids. They had lost everything.

_____

HIT THE SPOT

to be just right, to be refreshing

[dar placer]

> The dessert was perfect. It hit the spot.

_____

MAKE A HIT

to get appreciation, approval, success

[ganar aprobación]

> Jessica's hairdo made a hit at the party.

_____

HOCUS-POCUS

HOCUS-POCUS

magic tricks used for deception

[trucos para decepcionar]

> There has been some hocus-pocus in these accounts to try to confuse the accountant.

_____

HOG

LIVE HIGH OFF THE **HOG***

ROAD* HOG

HOGWASH

HOGWASH

nonsense

[tonterías]

> Etta's story about her trip is a lot of hogwash. She never left home.

_____

HOLD

CAN'T HOLD A **CANDLE*** TO

HOLD AT **BAY***

HOLD ONE'S TONGUE

to refrain from saying something

[callarse]

> I held my tongue during the argument, though I had much to say.

_____

HOLD OUT

(1) to wait

[esperar]

> John held out for a promotion on the job, instead of moving to another company.

_____

(2) to last or endure

[durar]

> There is very little fuel in our tank. I hope it holds out until we get to a gas station.

_____

HOLD OVER; HOLD SOMETHING OR SOMEONE OVER

(1) to remain in the same grade one more time

[hacerle repetir un grado a un niño]

> Joe was held over in the first grade because he needed more time there. The school held Joe over.

_____

(2) to be postponed for another time

[retener algo para otro tiempo]

> At the teachers' meeting, the discussion about the science lesson was held over for the next time. The chairperson held the discussion over.

71

HOLD UP
   See **HELD*** UP.
HOLD YOUR HORSES! (NOTE: NO VARIATION!)
   Wait!
   [¡Espérate! ¡Espére (n) se!]
    Hold your horses! Don't start your project until the plans are ready.

HOLDING
   BE LEFT HOLDING THE **BAG***

HOLE
   BURN* A HOLE IN ONE'S POCKET

HOLES
   SHOOT **FULL*** OF HOLES

HOME
   BRING HOME THE **BACON***
   TILL THE COWS **COME*** HOME
   EAT* ONE OUT OF HOUSE AND HOME

HOOK, HOOKY
   BY HOOK OR BY **CROOK***
   HOOK, LINE AND SINKER
    completely
    [enteramente]
     Mr. Martin believed the used car salesman's explanation of how all the defects were taken care of. He swallowed the story hook, line and sinker.

   OFF THE HOOK
    without further responsibility
    [sin más responsabilidad]
     Slim has been cleared of the charge of stealing the bicycle. He is finally off the hook.

   PLAY HOOKY
    to take unauthorized leave from school or a job
    [hacer novillos]

In New York City, the police are now looking for young people who play hooky from school instead of attending.

HOP
   HOP TO IT!
    Begin! Move quickly!
    [¡Andale! ¡Andele!]
     We're about to start jogging. Hop to it!

HORNS
   TAKE THE **BULL*** BY THE HORNS

HORSE
   DARK* HORSE
   DON'T LOOK A **GIFT*** HORSE IN THE MOUTH
   FOOL*, MESS, HORSE AROUND
   HORSE OF ANOTHER **COLOR***
   HORSE SENSE
    common sense
    [sentido común]
     Not only is he a learned man, but he also has a lot of horse sense. He can be quite practical.

   ON ONE'S HIGH HORSE
    arrogant
    [arrogante]
     When we ask him to help with the dishes, he gets on his high horse and says that he has better things to do.

   ONE-HORSE TOWN
    small town with very few facilities
    [un pueblo pequeño con pocos recursos culturales]
     People in this one-horse town have very different lifestyles from those in the big cities.

   PUT THE **CART*** BEFORE THE HORSE

---

*Look under the **key word*** for this idiom.

STRAIGHT FROM THE HORSE'S MOUTH
from the authoritative source
[de un origen de autoridad]
> *Selma got it straight from the horse's mouth that there would only be a half day of school on Thursday.*

HORSES
HOLD* YOUR HORSES

HOT
BLOW HOT AND **COLD***
GET HOT UNDER THE **COLLAR***
HOT **AIR***
ON THE HOT SEAT
in a difficult position
[en una situación difícil]
> *The policeman accused of bias is on the hot seat.*

HOTSHOT
an expert
[un perito]
> *Zoe will clear up our computer problems. She is a computer hotshot.*

IN HOT **WATER***
NOT SO HOT
not good
[no muy bueno]
> *Don't see that movie. It is not so hot.*

SELL* LIKE HOTCAKES
STRIKE WHILE THE IRON IS HOT
to do something when the time is right
[hacer uno su agosto]
> *Charles has some free time now, so I must strike while the iron is hot and ask him to help me with my work.*

HOUR
ELEVENTH* HOUR

HOUSE
BRING* DOWN THE HOUSE
EAT* ONE OUT OF HOUSE AND HOME
FULL HOUSE
(1) a hall or auditorium filled to capacity
[un auditorio totalmente lleno de público]
> *Pavarotti sang to a full house. Every seat was taken.*

(2) in poker, three cards of a kind and a pair
[en póker, tres cartas del mismo valor y dos cartas de otro]
> *Paul won this round of poker with a full house. He had three jacks and two eights.*

IN THE **DOGHOUSE***
KEEP HOUSE
to take care of the household duties
[estar encargado de las tareas de la casa]
> *After his work, Maury helps Martha keep house.*

ON THE HOUSE
free of charge
[gratis]
> *In restaurants in the U. S., bread and butter are on the house.*

73

HUDDLE

GO INTO A HUDDLE

to confer privately in a small group

[conferir privadamente en un grupo pequeño]

The sales team went into a huddle to plan their next strategy.

HUMBLE

EAT HUMBLE PIE (EAT CROW*)

HUNG

HUNG UP ON

See **HANG-UP.**

HUNGER

FROM HUNGER

unsatisfactory, bad

[no satisfactorio]

That paint job is from hunger. It has already started to peel.

ICE

BREAK* THE ICE

SKATE ON THIN ICE

to take a risk

[ser osado]

Rafi was skating on thin ice when he played with fireworks. They are dangerous.

ILL

ILL AT EASE*

IMAGE

SPITTING IMAGE

look alike

[una cosa o una persona que es del mismo parecer como otra]

The twins are spitting images of each other.

INSANE

DRIVE ONE CRAZY* (INSANE)

INSIDE

KNOW SOMETHING INSIDE-OUT

to understand something thoroughly

[conocer algo perfectamente]

Marty knows his subject inside-out.

IRON

IRON CURTAIN*

IRON OUT SOMETHING; IRON SOMETHING OUT

to remove problems or differences

[quitar problemasa o diferencias]

Mabel and Jerry get along very well; they iron out all their differences as soon as they arise.

STRIKE WHILE THE IRON IS HOT*

IRONS

HAVE MANY IRONS IN THE FIRE*

ITSY-BITSY

ITSY-BITSY

tiny

[pequeñísimo]

An itsy-bitsy insect was crawling on the wall. It was almost invisible.

JACK

BEFORE YOU CAN* SAY JACK ROBINSON

JACK-OF-ALL-TRADES

one who can do many things

[factótum]

It is helpful to know a jack-of-all-trades who can repair things in the house.

JACK UP SOMETHING; JACK SOMETHING UP

to raise something, including prices

[alzar algo, precios inclusos]

The service station jacked up the price of repairing the car.

JAM

JAM-PACKED

crowded

[atestado]

The theatre was so jam-packed that the fire marshalls requested that some people leave.

[blank box]

IN A JAM (NOTE: JAM MAY HAVE A MODIFIER, SUCH AS BIG, TERRIBLE)

in trouble

[en apuros]

Leonard is in a big jam because he can't get back to work on time, and his boss is already there, waiting for him.

[blank box]

JERKER

TEAR* JERKER

JITTERS

HAVE THE JITTERS

to be frightened

[tener miedo]

Sam had the jitters while he waited for the doctor to tell him whether he had AIDS.

[blank box]

JOB

DEAD* END JOB

GIVE* ONE A SNOW JOB

JOHN

JOHN **HANCOCK***

JOINT

CASE THE JOINT

to inspect a place before using it

[inspeccionar un lugar antes de utilizarlo]

I want to case the joint before renting it for the party, to be sure it is suitable.

[blank box]

CLIP* JOINT

NOSE OUT OF JOINT

feeling offended

[estando ofendido]

Lucy's nose was out of joint because I did not make a birthday party for her.

[blank box]

JOKE

CRACK* A JOKE

JONESES

KEEP UP WITH THE JONESES

to try to live at the same level as one's community; to compete

[tratar de vivir al mismo nivel como el de los vecinos]

After Anne saw how modern Betsy's kitchen was, she decided to redo her kitchen the same way. She wants to keep up with the Joneses.

[blank box]

JOT

JOT DOWN SOMETHING; JOT SOMETHING DOWN

to make a written note of

[apuntar, escribir]

I forgot to jot his name down.

[blank box]

JUMP

JUMP AT

to seize an opportunity

[aprovecharse de una oportunidad]

I jumped at the chance to visit my grandmother in Toledo.

[blank box]

JUMP DOWN SOMEONE'S **THROAT***

JUMP (CLIMB,GET) ON THE **BANDWAGON***

JUMP THE **GUN***

JUST

JUST UNDER THE **WIRE***

KEEP

KEEP A STIFF UPPER **LIP***

KEEP AN **EYE*** ON

KEEP AT IT

to continue to do what one is doing; to persevere

[seguir con lo que uno está haciendo]

*Look under the **key word*** for this idiom.

Your daily exercise strengthens your muscles. Keep at it!

_____

KEEP **GOOD*** TIME
KEEP **HOUSE***
KEEP IN TOUCH
  to remain in contact
  [mantener comunicación]
    Sam and Harry kept in touch by telephone and fax machine.

_____

KEEP ONE'S **CHIN*** UP
KEEP ONE'S FINGERS **CROSSED***
KEEP ONE'S **HEAD***
KEEP ONE'S **HEAD*** ABOVE WATER
KEEP ONE'S NOSE **CLEAN***
KEEP ONE'S NOSE TO THE **GRINDSTONE***
KEEP **PLUGGING*** AWAY
KEEP SOMEONE **COMPANY***
KEEP SOMEONE IN **LINE***
KEEP SOMETHING UNDER ONE'S **HAT***
KEEP THE **BALL*** ROLLING
KEEP THE WOLF FROM THE **DOOR***
KEEP **TRACK*** OF
KEEP UP WITH THE **JONESES***

KETTLE
A FINE KETTLE OF **FISH***
POT **CALLING*** THE KETTLE BLACK

KICK
TO BELLYACHE, **BEEF***, GRIPE, KICK, SQUAWK
TO GET A KICK, **BANG***, CHARGE, OUT OF
KICK A **HABIT***
KICK IN THE PANTS (TEETH)
  an undeserved and harmful criticism or event
  [crítica o comportamiento que causa desaliento a alguien]
    After Mary spent time repairing the teacher's computer, Mary was criticized by the teacher for not doing her lesson. This was really a kick in the pants (teeth).

_____

KICK ONESELF FOR
  to regret
  [sentir]

I could kick myself for not buying that dress last week. When I went back for it, it was gone.

_____

KICK SOMETHING AROUND; KICK AROUND SOMETHING
  to discuss something
  [conferenciar sobre algo]
    We kicked around the idea of sharing a summer house on the beach, and finally decided we would do it. It was helpful to kick the idea around.

_____

KICK THE **BUCKET***
KICK UP A **FUSS***

KID
HANDLE WITH KID **GLOVES***
KID AROUND
  to joke, to play
  [bromear, jugar]
    We kidded around for about an hour before settling down to serious work.

_____

KIDDING
YOU'RE KIDDING! (Note: No variation!)
  You are joking!
  [¡Habla(-s,-n), en broma!]
    You're kidding! I don't believe that you built that beautiful table with the few tools you have.

_____

KILL
KILL TWO **BIRDS*** WITH ONE STONE

KILLING
MAKE A KILLING (NOTE: KILLING MAY HAVE MODIFIER)
  to earn a lot of money quickly
  [ganar mucho dinero rapidamente]
    Andrew made a killing when the price of the coffee in his warehouse went up and he sold two tons of it.

_____

KISS

KISS SOMETHING **GOODBYE***

KITE

GO **FLY*** A KITE

KNIFE

GO* UNDER THE KNIFE

KNOCK

KNOCK IT OFF! (Note: No variation!)

Stop!

[¡Dejalo! ¡Deje(n)lo!]

> *Pat told them "Knock it off." Their noise was irritating her.*

_____

KNOCK OFF

to quit

[cesar]

> *We knocked off work early to go to the beach.*

_____

KNOCK ONE **DEAD***

KNOCK ONE FOR A LOOP

to surprise one

[sorprenderle a uno}

> *Seeing my father in the principal's office knocked me for a loop. I was upset all day.*

_____

KNOCK ONE'S HEAD AGAINST THE WALL

to make a useless attempt to do something

[tratar de hacer algo sin éxito]

> *I knocked my head against the wall trying to solve that algebra problem, but I never succeeded.*

_____

KNOCK ONESELF OUT

(1) to try very hard

[echar muchos esfuerzos]

> *I knocked myself out to finish that job on time.*

_____

(2) to become exhausted

[ponerse una persona agotada]

> *I knocked myself out with all that exercise.*

_____

KNOCKOUT

(1) a very attractive person

[persona muy hermosa]

> *All eyes are on Mamie. She's a knockout!*

_____

(2) a blow in a sport fight that knocks the opponent down for 10 seconds

[noqueada]

> *Ali has won 60 of his 70 fights by knockouts.*

_____

KNOT

TIE THE KNOT

to get married

[casarse]

> *Joe and Sally finally tied the knot last year. They were married in June.*

_____

KNOW

KNOW BY **SIGHT***

KNOW IF ONE IS **COMING*** OR GOING

KNOW SOMETHING **INSIDE*** OUT

KNOW THE ROPES

to be experienced

[tener experiencia]

> *Adrian will answer all your questions on this job. She knows the ropes.*

_____

YOU* KNOW

KNOW-HOW

KNOW-HOW

expertise

[pericia]

*Look under the **key word*** for this idiom.

When you've been on this job as long as Aaron, you will have the same know-how.

L - M - N - O - P - Q

LAME
LAME **DUCK***

LAND
LAND ON ONE'S **FEET***

LARGE
BY AND LARGE
usually
[usualmente]
> *By and large, boys are bigger boned than girls.*

LASHING
GIVE* ONE A TONGUE LASHING

LAST
BE ON ITS LAST LEGS
to be ready to stop functioning
[estar algo para dejar de funcionar]
> *The old sewing machine I inherited from my mother is on its last legs.*

THE LAST **LAUGH***

THE LAST STRAW
the final insult or injury, after which one can endure no more
[la última injuria, tras la cual no se soporta más]
> *Receiving that nasty letter from Jim was the last straw. We are no longer friends.*

LAUGH
LAUGH UP ONE'S SLEEVE
to be amused secretly
[reírse con disimulo]
> *Tom bragged that the company was going to send him to California. Mel laughed up his sleeve because he knew that there was no money for the trip.*

HAVE THE LAST LAUGH
to be finally proved correct; to laugh at someone who has laughed at you
[la satisfacción de saber que uno tiene se ha razón; reirse uno de alguien que se ha reído de él]
> *Jim laughed when I fell on the ice, but I had the last laugh when his pants ripped at the seam.*

LAUGHING
BURST* OUT LAUGHING

LAUNDRY
AIR* ONE'S DIRTY LINEN (LAUNDRY) IN PUBLIC

LAW
LAY DOWN THE LAW
to announce the rules emphatically and without question
[anunciar las reglas de una manera definitiva]
> *My father laid down the law about wearing a seat-belt while driving.*

LAY
LAY AN **EGG***

LAY DOWN THE **LAW***

LAY IT ON THE LINE
to speak very firmly about something
[hablar con firmeza]
> *She laid it on the line. There was to be no more fighting or we would lose all of our privileges.*

LAY (PUT, **POUR***, SPREAD) IT ON THICK

LAY OFF SOMEONE
to leave someone alone
[dejar en paz a alguien]

*Look under the **key word*** for this idiom.

Lay off Terry. You've bothered him too much already.

LAY (PUT) ONE'S **CARDS*** ON THE TABLE

LAY SOMEONE OFF

to dismiss someone from a job (sometimes temporarily)

[despedir a alguien de su empleo (permanente o temporalmente)]

The boss laid off six seamstresses during the slow season.

LAY SOMETHING ON SOMEONE

to blame someone

[echarle la culpa a alguien]

Don't lay that explosion on me! I was nowhere near the place when it happened.

LEAD

LEAD SOMEONE AROUND BY THE NOSE

to have full control over someone

[controlar a alguien completamente]

Glenn admits that Sylvia leads him around by the nose. But he does not feel bad about it.

LEAF

TURN OVER A NEW LEAF

to change one's behavior for the better

[mejorar uno su manera de ser]

Rafi turned over a new leaf. He stopped complaining and became more agreeable.

LEARN

LEARN BY **HEART***

LEARN THE ROPES

to learn the skills and procedures on a job or project

[aprender las habilidades para un trabajo o un proyecto]

Julie learned the ropes very quickly on her new job as a receptionist.

LEFT

FROM LEFT **FIELD***

LEFT HOLDING THE **BAG***

OUT IN LEFT **FIELD***

LEFT-HANDED

LEFT-HANDED **COMPLIMENT***

LEG

(COST) AN **ARM*** AND A LEG

NOT TO HAVE A LEG TO STAND ON

to have no reasonable support in a dispute

[no tener ningún apoyo en una disputa]

Van had no leg to stand on in asking the teacher to raise his grade from B to A. He missed almost half of the classes.

PULL SOMEONE'S LEG

to tease with a playful lie

[tomarle a uno el pelo]

Paul takes everything seriously. He never knows when I'm pulling his leg by saying something ridiculous, because I seem serious even though I am joking.

. **SHAKE A LEG!** (NOTE: NO VARIATION!)

Hurry!

[¡Date (Dé(n)se) prisa!]

Shake a leg! We want to be at the theatre before the curtain goes up!

LEGS

ON ITS **LAST*** LEGS

LEND

LEND AN **EAR***

LET

LET **BYGONES*** BE BYGONES

NOT TO LET GRASS GROW UNDER ONE'S **FEET***

LET IT ALL HANG OUT
  to reveal everything
  [revelar todo]
    The couple told us all about their marital
    problems. They let it all hang out.

```


```

LET (**BLOW***) OFF STEAM

LET ON
  to reveal that one knows something
  [revelar que uno sabe algo]
    Karli let on that she knew her mother was
    planning a surprise birthday party for her.

```


```

LET ONE'S HAIR DOWN; LET DOWN ONE'S HAIR
  to relax and speak frankly
  [relajarse y hablar de asuntos íntimos]
    Kathy let her hair down and talked about her
    most intimate fears.

```


```

LET SOMEONE DOWN; LET DOWN SOMEONE
  to disappoint someone
  [desilusionar a alguien]
    Lynn promised to help Marty but she let him
    down when she did not show up to help him.

```


```

LET SOMEONE HAVE IT
  to attack someone physically or verbally
  [atacar a alguien física o verbalmente]
    Marty let Lynn have it when she did not deliver
    on her promises.

```


```

LET SOMEONE OFF; LET OFF SOMEONE
  (1) to excuse someone from a punishment
  [perdonar a alguien sin castigo]
    Nathan was let off with no penalty because
    this was his first offense.

```


```

  (2) to permit someone to get out of a vehicle
  [permitir a alguien bajar de un vehículo]
    The bus let Grace off one block from her home.

```


```

LET SOMETHING RIDE
  to leave a situation as it is
  [dejar una situación como tal]
    I was going to have the kitchen repainted, but
    I decided to let it ride until next year.

```


```

LET SOMETHING SLIDE
  to neglect something
  [descuidar algo]
    Millie let the homework slide while she
    praticed for her driving exam.

```


```

LET THE CAT OUT OF THE **BAG***

LET THE **CHIPS*** FALL WHERE THEY MAY

LET UP
  to lessen the intensity
  [disminuir la intensidad]
    If this rain doesn't let up soon, we will all be
    soaking wet.

```


```

LETTER
RED LETTER **DAY***

LEVEL
ON THE LEVEL
  honest
  [franco]
    Jules was on the level when he told of his
    wartime fears. He never lies.

```


```

*Look under the **key word*** for this idiom.

LICK

A LICK AND A PROMISE

a small amount

[un poquito]

Martha didn't have time to give the apartment a complete cleaning. She didn't: she just gave it a lick and a promise.

LID

FLIP* ONE'S LID; FLIP OUT

LIFE

GET* A LIFE

LIFE OF THE PARTY

an interesting, outgoing person

[una persona interesante y amigable]

It is always fun to be with Rita; with her sense of humor, she's the life of the party.

LIVE THE LIFE OF RILEY

to live a comfortable life without worries

[tener una vida cómoda sin preocupaciones]

He intends to live the life of Riley when he retires. We wish him luck.

NOT ON YOUR LIFE

absolutely not

[de ninguna manera]

I refuse to appear on a foolish TV talk show. Not on your life!

LIKE

LIKE **FALLING*** OFF A LOG

TELL* IT LIKE IT IS

LIMB

GO OUT ON A LIMB

assume a risky position

[estar en un atolladero]

I went out on a limb and said I would track down the car-jacker.

LINE

DRAW* THE LINE

DROP* SOMEONE A LINE

GET* OUT OF LINE

HOOK*, LINE AND SINKER

KEEP SOMEONE IN LINE

to get someone to behave in an acceptable way

[hacer que alguien se conforme]

Ronald disrupted the class many times. Finally, he was transferred to a teacher who would keep him in line.

LAY* IT ON THE LINE

STEP (**GET***) OUT OF LINE

LINEN

AIR* ONE'S DIRTY LINEN IN PUBLIC

LINES

READ BETWEEN THE LINES

to find the hidden meaning

[comprender lo ocultado en las palabras expresadas]

Dorothy says that she enjoys going to the art class, but I read between the lines, from the expression on her face, that she would prefer not to go.

LION'S

THE LION'S SHARE

the biggest share

[la porción más grande]

The man who invested the money took the lion's share of the profits, even though he did none of the work.

LIP

BUTTON* ONE'S LIP

KEEP A STIFF UPPER LIP

to remain calm and courageous

[mantenerse tranquilo]

Rhoda kept a stiff upper lip while waiting for the names of the survivors of the plane crash. Her sister was one of the passengers.

ZIP ONE'S LIP
to keep a secret
[mantener un secreto]
I promised to zip my lip when he told me to keep his credit card number a secret.

LIVE
LIVE **HIGH*** OFF THE HOG
LIVE IT UP
to have a good time
[divertirse]
When he got that raise in pay, Joe decided to live it up a bit. He took his wife to an expensive restaurant.

LIVE THE **LIFE*** OF RILEY
A LIVE WIRE
an active, alert person
[una persona viva]
Tom will be an excellent salesman; he's a live wire.

LOADED
TO BE LOADED
to have a lot of money
[tener mucho dinero]
Jim was loaded when he entered the gambling casino. When he left, he was down to his last dollar.

LOCAL
LOCAL YOKEL
one who has limited experience and is not sophisticated
[un rustico]

The local yokels in this neighborhood will not appreciate this opera. They are not cultured.

LOCK
LOCK, STOCK AND **BARREL***

LOG
LIKE **FALLING*** OFF A LOG
SIT THERE LIKE A **BUMP*** ON A LOG

LONG
IN THE LONG RUN
eventually
[con tiempo]
In the long run, exercise is better than drugs for the heart.

LOOK
DIRTY* LOOK
DON'T LOOK A **GIFT*** HORSE IN THE MOUTH

LOOK DOWN ON
to regard as inferior
[menospreciar]
Young people nowadays tend to look down on the aged and infirm.

LOOK DOWN ONE'S NOSE AT
to regard as inferior with contempt

*Look under the **key word*** for this idiom.

[despreciar]

Harley-Davidson motorcycle owners look down their noses at other motorbikes. They do not think other motorbikes are good.

_____

LOONEY

LOONY-BIN

insane asylum; mental hospital

[manicomio]

Everyone here is acting strangely agitated; the place reminds me of a looney-bin.

_____

LOOP

KNOCK* ONE FOR A LOOP

LOOSE

BREAK* LOOSE

HANG* LOOSE

HAVE A **SCREW*** LOOSE

LOSE

LOSE ONE'S **COOL***

LOSE ONE'S **HEAD***

LOSE ONE'S MARBLES

to lose one's mental faculties

[perder el juicio]

When she came to the office wearing an evening gown, people in the office thought that she was losing her marbles.

_____

LOSE ONE'S SHIRT

to lose all of one's money

[perder uno todo su dinero]

Henry lost his shirt betting at the races last night.

_____

LOSE ONE'S **TEMPER***

LOSE ONE'S TOUCH

to lose one's skill

[perder la habilidad]

I've lost my touch in baking. I've neglected it for too long.

_____

LOSE TRACK OF SOMEONE

not to know where someone else is

[no saber uno donde está otra persona]

I've lost track of all of my high school buddies.

_____

LOSER

SORE LOSER

one who is bad tempered when he loses

[alguien que siempre está resentido al perder un juego, una discusión, etc.]

I hate to play with Al. He is a sore loser.

_____

LOST

GET* LOST

LOT

COVER* A LOT OF GROUND

HAVE A LOT ON THE **BALL***

IT'S A LOT OF **BALONEY***

LOUSE

MESS, LOUSE, **FOUL*** UP SOMETHING

LOUSY

FEEL LOUSY

to feel bad

[sentirse mal]

I felt lousy before and after taking that medication.

_____

LOVE

HEAD* OVER HEELS IN LOVE

LOWER

LOWER THE **BOOM*** ON SOMEONE

LYING

TAKE SOMETHING LYING DOWN

to accept something unpleasant without resistance

[aceptar algo desagradable sin resistir]

Ralph refused to take that cut in pay lying down. He used a good argument, and won.

_____

MADE

HAVE IT MADE

to have everything needed for success

[tener todo lo necesario para tener éxito]

Tom was a star in a Broadway show. He has it made.

MAKE

MAKE A **BUNDLE***

MAKE A CLEAN **BREAK***

MAKE A CLEAN **BREAST***

MAKE A **DENT*** IN

MAKE A FEDERAL **CASE*** OUT OF SOMETHING

MAKE A GO OF

to succeed in, to get good results from

[tener éxito en]

They are working very hard to make a go of their new restaurant.

MAKE A **HIT***

MAKE A **KILLING***

MAKE A MOUNTAIN OUT OF A MOLEHILL

to exaggerate the importance of a small problem

[exagerar la importancia de un problema pequeño]

When I spilled a drop of milk on her blouse, Etta screamed at me and made a mountain out molehill.

MAKE A PITCH FOR

to make a statement promoting something, or asking for money for something

[pregonar para promover algo o pedir dinero por]

Before the curtain went up, one of the actors appeared on stage and made a pitch for contributions to the theatre.

MAKE **BELIEVE***

MAKE **CLEAR***

MAKE **ENDS*** MEET

MAKE **EYES*** AT

MAKE **FACES***

MAKE **GOOD*** TIME

MAKE IT UP TO SOMEONE

to compensate someone

[compensar a alguien]

Abbie cried when Debbie left in the morning. She made it up to her by taking her to the playground in the afternoon.

MAKE IT **SNAPPY***

MAKE NO **BONES*** ABOUT

MAKE ONE'S **BLOOD*** BOIL

MAKE ONE'S HAIR STAND ON **END***

MAKE ONE'S MOUTH WATER

to make someone hungry

[hacerse la boca agua]

Looking at those pickles makes my mouth water. I can't wait to eat one.

MAKE ONE'S OWN WAY

to act independently

[actuar independientemente]

He left home as a teenager, got a job and an apartment, and, from then on, made his own way in life.

MAKE ONESELF SCARCE

to go away; to be unavailable

[irse; estar inaccesible]

My roommate became very angry, and I decided that it was best to make myself scarce. I went to the library to study.

MAKE OUT LIKE A **BANDIT***

MAKE SOMEONE OR SOMETHING TICK

to make someone or something work properly

[hacer funcionar bien a alguien o algo]

He took the motor apart to see what makes it tick. He learned how to repair it.

85

*Look under the **key word*** for this idiom.

MAKE UP; MAKE UP SOMETHING; MAKE SOMETHING UP
(1) to make peace after a quarrel
[hacer las paces]

> *Sally and Sue had an argument, but now talk to each other. They made up after their quarrel.*

_____

(2) to fabricate; to tell a story that is not based on reality
[inventar]

Linda has a fantastic imagination, and makes up interesting stories all the time. She will be a writer.

_____

MAKE-UP
cosmetics usually applied to the face
[maquillaje]

> *Mary wears make-up every day. She puts it on before she goes to school.*

_____

MAKE UP ONE'S MIND
to make a decision
[decidir]

> *Hedi made up her mind to be a librarian.*

_____

MAKE WAVES
to disturb a situation
[alborotar una situación]

> *When Jason became the coach of the football team, he made everyone practice every day! He certainly made waves on the team!*

_____

MAN
MAN-TO-MAN
as equals
[a nivel de iguales]

> *Forget that I am your father. I'd like to speak with you man-to-man. What are your intentions about looking for a job and supporting yourself?*

_____

RIGHT-**HAND*** MAN

MANNERS
MIND ONE'S MANNERS
to behave properly
[comportarse bien]

> *Mother told Kate to mind her manners when*

_____

> *she had dinner with her friend's family.*

MARBLES
LOSE* ONE'S MARBLES

MARKET
IN THE MARKET FOR SOMETHING
ready to buy something
[al punto de comprar algo]

_____

> *I am finally in the market for a CD player.*

PLAY THE MARKET
to gamble in the stockmarket with stocks and bonds
[jugar invirtiendo en la bolsa de valores]

> *Joe doesn't have enough money to play the market. He keeps his money in the bank.*

_____

MATTER
NO MATTER
(1) never mind; not important
[no importa]

> *Did you leave your library card at home? No matter, we can borrow the books with my card.*

(2) regardless of, in spite of

_____

[a pesar de]

> *No matter what you say, I still think that dress looks good on me.*

MAY

LET THE CHIPS* FALL WHERE THEY MAY

MC COY

THE REAL MCCOY

the genuine thing

[la cosa original o auténtica]

That cowboy hat is the real McCoy. It was given to me by a working cowboy.

MEAN

TO MEAN **BUSINESS***

MEDICINE

GIVE SOMEONE A DOSE (TASTE) OF ONE'S OWN MEDICINE

to treat someone in the same unpleasant way as that person has treated you

[reciprocar uno la maldad que otro le ha hecho]

I raised my voice to her, just as she had done to me. I gave her a taste of her own medicine.

MEET

MAKE **ENDS*** MEET

MEET ONE **HALFWAY***

MESS

FOOL*, MESS, HORSE AROUND

MESS, LOUSE, **FOUL*** UP SOMETHING

MILL

BE **THROUGH*** THE MILL

RUN-OF-THE-MILL

mediocre, ordinary

[corriente, ordinario]

They sold run-of-the-mill T-shirts at the flea market. There was nothing worth buying.

MIND

BEAR* IN MIND

BLOW* ONE'S MIND

BOGGLE* THE MIND (MIND-BOGGLING)

BOMBED* OUT OF ONE'S MIND OR SKULL

BRING* TO MIND

CHANGE* ONE'S MIND

CROSS* ONE'S MIND

GIVE* A PIECE OF ONE'S MIND

HAVE A MIND OF ONE'S OWN

to think independently

[pensar independientemente]

This two year old is remarkable. He already has a mind of his own.

BE IN ONE'S RIGHT MIND

to be sane, sensible

[estar cuerdo]

Sal was not in his right mind when he agreed to pay $300 to repair the dented fender. The cost should have been under $100.

MAKE* UP ONE'S MIND

MIND ONE'S **MANNERS***

MIND ONE'S OWN BUSINESS

to refrain from intruding in the affairs of others

[no entrometerse en los asuntos de otras personas]

Ben, don't ask me so many questions. Mind your own business.

MIND ONE'S P'S AND Q'S

to behave properly

[comportarse bien]

Mind your P's and Q's when you visit the White House with your class. Be polite; do as you're told.

MIND THE STORE

to take care of things

[ocuparse uno de sus asuntos]

When my mother went to Chicago, I minded the store. I made a record of all the messages and phone calls.

*Look under the **key word*** for this idiom.

ONE-TRACK MIND

a mind that can deal with only one thing at a time
[la capacidad de poder pensar solamente en un asunto]

Paul talks only about the problems caused by inflation. He has a one-track mind.

BE OUT OF ONE'S MIND

to be insane, crazy
[estar loco]

He is out of his mind if he thinks I will work this weekend.

PUT SOMETHING OUT OF ONE'S MIND (HEAD*)

SLIP ONE'S MIND

to forget
[escapar de la memoria de alguién]

My two o'clock appointment with Mindy slipped my mind. I forgot all about it.

MINE

GOLD* MINE

MISS

NOT MISS A TRICK

to observe everything
[observar todo]

The salesman tried to substitute another ring in place of the one she had bought, but Janet did not miss a trick. She saw him do it.

MISS THE BOAT*

MOLEHILL

MAKE* A MOUNTAIN OUT OF A MOLEHILL

MONEY

STRAPPED* FOR MONEY

MONKEY

GREASE* MONKEY

MONKEY AROUND WITH

to play with or to do something in a haphazard way
[manipular al azar]

Jack monkeyed around with the watch, but he was never able to get it to work.

MONKEY BUSINESS

underhandedness
[fraude]

The answers on two exam papers are so much alike that there must have been some monkey business. I think one of the students cheated.

MOOCH

MOOCH

to beg shamelessly
[gorrear]

Sal mooched all of his meals. He made up a sad story about how poor he was, so he never had to pay for them.

MOOLAH

MOOLAH

money
[dinero]

Everyone knew that Pat had plenty of moolah. He loved to buy expensive clothing.

MOON

ONCE IN A BLUE* MOON
SEND SOMEONE TO THE MOON (INTO ORBIT*)

MORE

BITE* OFF MORE THAN ONE CAN CHEW

MOUNTAIN

MAKE* A MOUNTAIN OUT OF A MOLEHILL

MOUTH

BAD*-MOUTH

BY WORD OF MOUTH
  told from person to person
  [por medio de comunicación oral]
  The Royal restaurant does not advertise.
  All of its patrons come by word of mouth.

DON'T LOOK A **GIFT*** HORSE IN THE MOUTH
HAND* TO MOUTH
MAKE* ONE'S MOUTH WATER
ONE'S **HEART*** IS IN ONE'S MOUTH
PUT ONE'S **FOOT*** IN ONE'S MOUTH
SHOOT ONE'S MOUTH OFF
  to talk too much, to reveal confidences
  [hablar indiscretamente]
  Jim shot his mouth off about the company's
  plan to merge with another company. This
  caused the value of its stock to drop.

TAKE THE WORDS OUT OF SOMEONE'S MOUTH
  to say something that someone else was going
  to say
  [decir lo que quería decir otra persona]
  Jennie and I looked at the painting in the
  museum. When she said, "I don't understand
  it," she took the words right out of my mouth.

MOUTHFUL
  SAY A MOUTHFUL
  to say something important or accurate
  [decir una cosa de importancia]
  Ruth certainly said a mouthful when she
  predicted that the Lennon memorial would
  be crowded.

MOVE
  GET* A MOVE ON

MUDSLINGING
  MUDSLINGING
  damage to someone's reputation
  [perjudicar la reputación de alguien]
  There has been more mudslinging at candidates
  in this election than ever before.

MUM
  MUM'S THE WORD. (DO NOT CONJUGATE!)
  Please keep this a secret.
  [Favor de mantener esto secreto.]
  Now that I've told you all of my personal
  problems, mum's the word. Do not discuss
  this with anyone.

MURDER
  GET* AWAY WITH MURDER
  YELL (SCREAM) **BLOODY*** MURDER

MUSIC
  FACE* THE MUSIC

NAIL
  FIGHT TOOTH AND NAIL
  to fight fiercely
  [luchar con ferocidad]
  Our candidate for Congress fought the opposition
  tooth and nail, and won.

HIT THE NAIL ON THE **HEAD***

NECK
  BREAK* ONE'S NECK
  PAIN IN THE NECK
  someone or something that is annoying
  [algo o alguien fastidioso]
  Harry talks too much. He is a pain in the neck.

STICK ONE'S NECK OUT
  to take a risk
  [arriesgarse]
  David stuck his neck out and volunteered to
  collect the firecrackers that had not exploded.

---

*Look under the **key word*** for this idiom.

NEEDLES

BE ON PINS AND NEEDLES

to be nervous, worried

[esta nervioso]

Andy was on pins and needles, waiting for the results of his father's surgery.

```
[empty box]
```

NERVES

GET* ON ONE'S NERVES

NEST

FEATHER* ONE'S NEST

NEST **EGG***

NEW

TURN OVER A NEW **LEAF***

NEWS

BREAK* THE NEWS

NICK

IN THE NICK OF TIME

just in time

[justo a tiempo]

Lily always gets to the theatre in the nick of time, just as the curtain goes up.

```
[empty box]
```

NIGHT

FLY* BY NIGHT

NIP

NIP IN THE **BUD***

NITPICK

TO NITPICK

to focus on trivial problems or errors

[ser melindroso]

Sophie's report misses the important points and nitpicks on unimportant details.

```
[empty box]
```

NITTY-GRITTY

NITTY-GRITTY

the basic details

[los detalles básicos]

After deciding on the dates for our vacation, we finally got down to the nitty-gritty of making the arrangements.

```
[empty box]
```

NO

NO **DICE***

NO **WAY***!

NOBODY

NOBODY'S **FOOL***

NOODLE

USE ONE'S NOODLE (**HEAD***)

NOSE

BROWN*-NOSE

FOLLOW* ONE'S NOSE

KEEP ONE'S NOSE **CLEAN***

KEEP ONE'S NOSE TO THE **GRINDSTONE***

LEAD* SOMEONE AROUND BY THE NOSE

LOOK* DOWN ONE'S NOSE AT

NOSE OUT OF **JOINT***

TO PAY THROUGH THE NOSE

to pay too much

[pagar un ojo de la cara]

I paid through the nose for that plane fare because it was the busy season.

```
[empty box]
```

RIGHT UNDER ONE'S NOSE

in an obvious place

[en un lugar obvio]

I hunted for my keys everywhere and finally found them on the table, right under my nose.

```
[empty box]
```

A RUNNING NOSE; ONE'S NOSE RUNS

a nose that drips mucus, frequently the result of a cold or an allergy

[una nariz de donde salen los mocos]

He has a running nose. He carries tissues all the time.

```
[empty box]
```

STICK ONE'S NOSE INTO

to intrude into, interfere with

[entremeterse en]

Manny is always sticking his nose into my business. He has very poor judgment.

NOTCH

TOP*-NOTCH

NOTHING

IN NOTHING **FLAT***

NOTHING **DOING***

NOTHING TO **SNEEZE*** AT

TO SAY NOTHING of

   plus, in addition to

   [además de]

     We expect two hundred adults at the wedding, to say nothing of the children.

NUMBER

HAVE SOMEONE'S NUMBER

   to know the kind of person someone is

   [saber cómo es una persona]

     He can't fool me. I've got his number.

TO PULL A NUMBER ON

   to cheat

   [engañar a]

     Jorge pulled a number on Philipe by giving him a broken radio for a good telephone.

NUT

HARD (TOUGH) NUT TO **CRACK***

NUTS

BE NUTS ABOUT

   to like very much, to love

   [estar loco por]

     I'm just nuts about jellybeans. I can eat them night and day.

NUTSHELL

IN A NUTSHELL

   in summary, briefly

   [en resumidas cuentas]

     The play was too long; the scenery was bad; the acting was poor. In a nutshell, the play is a failure.

ODDS

BE AT ODDS

   to be in disagreement

   [no estar de acuerdo]

     Sheila and Debby are at odds with each other because they are unhappy about the terms of the will.

ODDS AND **ENDS***

OFF

BUG* OFF

BUMP* OFF

COME* OFF IT

GET IT OFF YOUR **CHEST***; GET SOMETHING OFF ONE'S CHEST

OFF ONE'S **ROCKER***

WEAR* OFF

WELL* OFF

OINTMENT

FLY* IN THE OINTMENT

OLD

CHIP OFF THE OLD **BLOCK***

OLD **FLAME***

OLD **HAND***

OLD **HAT***

ON

CATCH* ON

ON THE **BALL***

ON THE **BANDWAGON***

ON THE **BLINK***

ON THE Q.T.

   secretly

   [a hurtadillas]

     Tom told his neighbor that he had no tickets to the ballgame, but he gave his brother Henry two tickets on the q.t.

*Look under the **key word*** for this idiom.

ON THE UP AND UP
honest, straightforward
[franco]
> *Mr. Jones is on the up and up when he describes the things he sells.*

ON THE **WHOLE***

ONCE
ONCE IN A **BLUE*** MOON
ONCE-OVER
careful examination
[examen cuidadoso]
> *Sarah gave the old crib the once-over before putting the baby in it.*

ONE
ONE FOR THE **BOOKS***
ONE FOR THE **ROAD***
ONE-**HORSE*** TOWN
ONE-TRACK **MIND***
SQUARE* ONE

OPEN
OPEN AND SHUT CASE
an outcome about which there is no doubt;
a situation that is clearly resolved
[una situación fácil de resolver]
> *The police had an open and shut case against Ike when they caught him with the stolen goods in his pocket.*

ORBIT
GO INTO ORBIT
to become ecstatic, very happy
[ponerse muy contento]
> *When Tanya learned that she had won the lottery, she went into orbit with joy.*

ORDER
APPLE*-PIE ORDER
OUT OF ORDER
(1) not in the correct sequence
[no en el orden correcto; fuera de servicio]
> *The pages in this book are out of order.*

(2) misbehaving
[fuera de control]
> *The teacher's voice cannot be heard because the class is out of order.*

(3) not working
[fuera de servicio]
> *This computer is out of order. It does not respond to directions.*

OUT
BAIL* ONE OUT
BE **CUT*** OUT TO BE
BE* OUT OF
BLOW*-OUT
BOMBED* OUT (OF ONE'S MIND OR SKULL)
BURN* ONESELF OUT; TO BE BURNED OUT
BUTT (**CHILL***) OUT
CLEAN* SOMEONE OUT
CLEAR* OUT
CONK* (ZONK) OUT
DISH* OUT
DROPOUT*
DOWN* AND OUT
EAT ONE'S **HEART*** OUT
HANG* OUT
BE OUT OF **DATE***
OUT OF SOMETHING
without, lacking something
[sin algo]
> *We're out of sugar again.*

BE OUT OF IT
to be confused and unable to concentrate

[confuso y sin el poder de concentrarse]
Don't be disappointed by Lon's strange response. He hasn't slept much and so he's out of it.

BE OUT OF ONE'S **MIND***
BE OUT OF **ORDER***
OUT OF THE **BLUE***
OUT OF THE **WOODS***
BE OUT OF THE **QUESTION***
BE OUT OF THIS **WORLD***
WORK* OUT
WEAR* OUT

OVER

BLOW* OVER
GET* OVER
ONCE*-OVER
OVER A **BARREL***
OVER ONE'S DEAD **BODY***
PUT* ONE OVER ON SOMEONE
TURN* over
TURN OVER A NEW **LEAF***
WALK* ALL OVER SOMEONE

P's

MIND* ONE'S P'S AND Q'S

PACKED

JAM* PACKED

PACKING

SEND SOMEONE PACKING
to tell someone to leave
[mandar salir a alguien]
After Tim accidentally spilled the paint into the machinery, his boss sent him packing.

PAD

PAD THE **BILL***

PAIN

NO **PAIN***, NO GAIN
GIVE* SOMEONE A PAIN
PAIN IN THE **NECK***

PAINS

TO TAKE PAINS
to be very careful, to work very hard

[poner cuidado especial]
Jim took great pains to hang the picture level.

PAINT

PAINT THE TOWN RED
to celebrate wildly; go on a spree.
[celebrar desenfrendamente]
Graduation was great. Now let's celebrate by going out tonight and painting the town red.

PALM

TO PALM SOMETHING OFF; TO PALM OFF SOMETHING
get rid of something in a dishonest way
[encajar algo de una manera deshonrada]
Jess palmed off that counterfeit twenty dollar bill at the grocery store check-out counter this morning.

PALSY-WALSY

TO BE PALSY-WALSY
friendly
[amigable]
Dan was palsy-walsy with Oscar in the third grade.

PAN

FLASH* IN THE PAN
OUT OF THE **FRYING*** PAN INTO THE FIRE
TO PAN OUT
to turn out all right
[salir bien]
Susie's plans for building a computer did not pan out this year.

PANCAKE

FLAT* AS A PANCAKE

PANKY

HANKY-**PANKY***

*Look under the **key word*** for this idiom.

PANTS

ANTS* IN ONE'S PANTS

BEAT* THE PANTS OFF (SOMONE)

KICK* IN THE PANTS (TEETH)

WEAR THE PANTS
> to have authority
> [tener la autoridad]
>> *In that family, Mary gives the orders.*
>> *She wears the pants.*

PAPERS

GIVE* ONE HIS/HER WALKING PAPERS

PAR

UP TO PAR
> at the normal standard
> [a la calidad normal]
>> *Mandy's cooking is not up to par.*

PART

TAKE PART IN
> to participate in
> [participar en]
>> *I was happy to take part in the game of vollyball.*

PARTY

LIFE* OF THE PARTY

PASS

PASS AWAY
> to die
> [fallecer]
>> *Ellen's mother passed away last year after a long illness.*

PASS OUT
> to faint
> [desmayarse]
>> *Rita passed out when she heard the bad news. Fortunately, she did not fall.*

PASS OUT THINGS
> to distribute things
> [distribuir cosas]
>> *Rosie passed out the test papers to the class.*

PASS THE **BUCK***

PASS WITH FLYING **COLORS***

PAUL

ROB PETER TO PAY PAUL
> to take from one in order to give to another
> [quitarle a uno para darle a otro]
>> *Lucy borrowed money from Nancy to return the money she had borrowed from Susan. She robbed Peter to pay Paul.*

PAVEMENT

POUND THE PAVEMENT
> to walk along the streets looking for something, usually looking for a job
> [caminar por los calles buscando algo, generalmente un empleo]
>> *Sima pounded the pavement for weeks looking for a job. All she found was other young people also looking for work.*

PAY

PAY A LEFT-HANDED **COMPLIMENT***

PAY THROUGH THE **NOSE***

ROB PETER TO PAY **PAUL***

PEDESTAL

PUT SOMEONE ON A PEDESTAL
> to idolize someone
> [idolatrar a alguien]
>> *During the sixties, young people certainly put Elvis Presley on a pedestal.*

PEP

A PEP TALK

speech to inspire enthusiasm and confidence
[un discurso para inspirar el entusiasmo y la
confianza]

*Joe gave me a pep talk before I went for
the job interview. It gave me courage.*

_____
_____

PERK

PERK UP

to elevate one's mood
[animar a alguien]

*I was feeling bad about not finding a job,
but hearing that song perked me up.*

_____
_____

PETER

ROB PETER TO PAY **PAUL***

PICK

BONE* TO PICK

PICK-ME-UP

a refreshing drink or snack
[una bebida o una merienda que refresca]

*I am hot, tired, and thirsty. I am going to have
a pick-me-up of cold orange juice.*

_____
_____

PICK UP THE **TAB***

PICNIC

NO PICNIC

not easy and not enjoyable
[penoso]

*Writing this composition is no picnic. It has
taken me four hours.*

_____
_____

PIE

A FINGER IN **EVERY*** PIE

APPLE*-PIE ORDER

EAT* HUMBLE PIE

PIE IN THE SKY

promise or hope that usually cannot be attained
[una promesa o una esperanza imposible de
lograr]

*They hired Jim as a mail clerk, and told him
that he might within a few years become a
partner. That is pie in the sky.*

_____
_____

PIECE

A PIECE OF **CAKE***

GIVE* SOMEONE A PIECE OF ONE'S MIND

PIECES

GO* TO PIECES

PIG

BUY* A PIG IN A POKE

PILLAR

FROM PILLAR TO POST

from one place to another
[de lugar en lugar]

*I searched from pillar to post for the book that
I needed.*

_____
_____

PIN

PIN SOMETHING ON SOMEONE

to place the blame for something on someone
[echarle la culpa a alguien]

*I was not there when the book disappeared,
so I could not have taken it. You can't pin
that on me.*

_____
_____

PINCH

IN A PINCH

if necessary
[en caso de necesidad]

*Our lawnmower is broken, but in a pinch I can
borrow one from our neighbor.*

_____
_____

*Look under the **key word*** for this idiom.

PINK

PINK SLIP

a notice that one is being dismissed from the job
[un aviso de despedida del empleo]

Many big companies give pink slips to employees when profits slip.

TICKLED PINK (SILLY)

delighted
[deleitado]

Joan loves the opera. She was tickled pink when a friend gave her opera tickets for her birthday.

PINS

ON PINS AND **NEEDLES***

PITCH

MAKE* A PITCH FOR

PITCH IN

to help, cooperate
[ayudar]

Max pitched in immediately to help move the piano.

PITCHING

BE IN THERE PITCHING

to be trying hard
[echando muchas fuerzas]

Ruth hates to scrub floors, but she's in there pitching with the rest of the clean-up crew.

PITS

THE PITS

very bad
[pesimo]

That shop is so hot in the summer that working there without air-conditioning during the summer is the pits.

PITY

TAKE PITY ON

to be sorry for
[compadecerse de]

Joel took pity on the old man standing near him in the subway, and gave him his seat.

PLACE

BETWEEN A ROCK AND A **HARD*** PLACE

ONE'S **HEART*** IS IN THE RIGHT PLACE

PUT IN ONE'S PLACE

to remind someone of his/her proper (usually lower) position
[acordar a alguien de su inferioridad]

Ann tried to take over my job at the meeting, but I put her in her place.

PLANET

ON THIS PLANET

practical and realistic
[práctico y realístico]

Ike thought he could buy a new car for $1,500.00. He is not on this planet.

PLAY

PLAY BY **EAR***

PLAY **HOOKY***

PLAY THE FIELD

to take advantage of many opportunities, rather than concentrating on one

Andy played the field while he was dating Marie. He went out with other women.

PLAY THE **MARKET***

PLAY SECOND **FIDDLE***

PLAY **TRICKS*** ON

PLAY UP TO SOMEONE

to flatter or try to please someone
[halagar a alguien]

Jules played up to all of his teachers, doing them favors, and hoping that that would help his grades.

PLAY WITH **FIRE***

PLEASED
TO BE PLEASED AS PUNCH
very satisfied
[muy satisfecho]
I was pleased as Punch when my guests enjoyed the dinner I had prepared.

PLUGGING
KEEP PLUGGING AWAY
to continue working at a project
[seguir trabajando en un proyecto]
I kept plugging away at the deskwork until all of the bills were paid.

PLUNGE
TAKE THE PLUNGE
to do something decisive, and perhaps risky
[hacer algo decisivo y un tanto arriesgado]
Bill and Leona finally took the plunge and got married.

POCKET
BURN* A HOLE IN ONE'S POCKET

POINT
BESIDE THE POINT
irrelevant
[fuera de propósito]
At the public hearing on rent control, Peter asked that the mail be placed properly in the mailboxes. That was beside the point.

STRETCH A POINT
to set aside the rules in order to be helpful
[ignorar las reglas para hacer un beneficio]
The library stretched a point and allowed Ezra to borrow the books for an extra week, without penalty.

POKE
BUY* A PIG IN A POKE

POLISHER
APPLE*-POLISHER

POOP
POOP
to defecate
[defecar]
Dogs should be prevented from pooping on the sidewalks in the city.

POOPED
POOPED
to be exhausted
[muy cansado]
I am absolutely pooped after moving the furniture. I will need an hour to rest.

POP
POP THE QUESTION
to ask someone to marry
[pedir la mano]
Tom popped the question last night, and Lucy agreed to marry him.

POST
FROM **PILLAR*** TO POST

POT
GO* TO POT
POT **CALLING*** THE KETTLE BLACK

POTTED
POTTED
drunk

*Look under the **key word*** for this idiom.

[borracho]
> *We can't discuss this problem with Clara until she is sober; after all the martinis she drank, she is potted.*

POUND
POUND THE **PAVEMENT***

POUR
TO POUR (SPREAD, PUT, LAY) IT ON THICK
to exaggerate
[exagerar]
> *Steve poured it on thick when he told of his bravery during the war.*

POWDER
TAKE A POWDER
to leave quickly
[esfumarse]
> *When I finally became tired and bored, I took a powder. I went home.*

PRETTY
SITTING PRETTY
to be in a good situation
[estar en una buena circunstancia]
> *Helen was sitting pretty after she inherited all that money.*

PROBLEM
SMOOTH* OVER A PROBLEM

PROMISE
A **LICK*** AND A PROMISE

PUBLIC
AIR* ONE'S DIRTY LINEN (LAUNDRY) IN PUBLIC

PULL
HAVE PULL (**CLOUT***, AN IN)
PULL A **BONER***

PULL A **FAST*** ONE
PULL ONESELF TOGETHER
to become calm
[calmarse]
> *After his angry outburst at the football team, the coach pulled himself together, calmed down, and explained what had gone wrong.*

PULL **PUNCHES***
PULL SOMEONE'S **LEG***
PULL SOMETHING OFF
to accomplish something unusual
[lograr hacer lo inusitado]
> *To everyone's surprise, Gregory pulled off the Houdini magic escape trick successfully.*

PULL **STRINGS***
PULL THE **RUG*** OUT FROM UNDER
PULL THE WOOL OVER ONE'S **EYES***
PULL UP STAKES
to relocate, to leave
[mudarse]
> *After five years in Toledo, Jack pulled up stakes and went to the far west.*

PUNCH
BEAT* SOMEONE TO THE PUNCH (DRAW)
PLEASED* AS PUNCH

PUNCHES
PULL ONE'S PUNCHES
to make a weak attack, physical or verbal
[no emplear toda la fuerza en un ataque]
> *Adele did not pull her punches when she scolded her younger sister for opening the door to a stranger.*

PURPOSE
SERVE SOMEONE'S PURPOSE
to be useful to someone
[ser util para una persona]

The potato masher will serve my purpose as well as the blender. All I want to do is mash the peas.

[   ]

PUSH

PUSH SOMEONE AROUND
to control someone
[controlar a alguien]
Tom requested a transfer to a different class. He was tired of the monitor's pushing him around all the time.

[   ]

PUT

PUT A **BUG*** IN ONE'S EAR
PUT A **DAMPER*** ON
PUT AN **END*** TO SOMETHING
PUT IN ONE'S TWO **CENTS*** WORTH
PUT (**POUR***, SPREAD, LAY) IT ON THICK
PUT ON WEIGHT
to gain weight
[subir de peso]
Missy is unhappy because she has put on a lot of weight. She looks very heavy.

[   ]

PUT ONE IN ONE'S **PLACE***
PUT ONE OVER ON SOMEONE
to deceive someone
[decepcionar a alguien]
Larry sure put one over on me. He promised to return my computer today, but he took it with him on vacation.

[   ]

PUT (LAY) ONE'S **CARDS*** ON THE TABLE
PUT ONE'S **FINGER*** ON
PUT ONE'S **FOOT*** DOWN
PUT ONE'S **FOOT*** IN ONE'S MOUTH
PUT OUR **HEADS*** TOGETHER
PUT OUT SOMEONE; PUT SOMEONE OUT
(1) to expel someone from someplace, usually home
[echar a alguien de la casa[
Mary put her son out of the house after he refused to give up his drug habit.

[   ]

(2) to cause inconvenience to someone
[incomodar a alguien]
I did not stay for dinner because I did not want to put Eliza out. She has a sick mother to take care of.

[   ]

PUT SOMEONE DOWN
(1) to criticize, or humiliate
[criticar o humillar a alguien]
Ella made an error in her composition, and the teacher put her down in front of the class. This was cruel.

[   ]

(2) to place one's name on a list
[inscribir a alguien en una lista]
May I put you down for a blood donation to the Red Cross?

[   ]

PUT SOMEONE ON
to fool, or tease someone
[engeñarle o tomarle el pelo a alguien]
He really doesn't mean it. He's just putting you on.

[   ]

PUT SOMEONE ON A **PEDESTAL***
PUT SOMETHING ACROSS
to explain or clarify something
[expresar algo]
Joe has trouble putting across how the machine works.

[   ]

PUT SOMETHING OUT OF ONE'S MIND (**HEAD***)

PUT SOMETHING OVER ON SOMEONE
to deceive someone
[decepcionar a alguien]
> *Len put something over on Marcus when he did not deliver the goods for which Marcus paid him.*

PUT THE BITE (TOUCH) ON SOMEONE
to try to borrow money from someone
[pedirle a alguien un préstamo de dinero]
> *Sally needed money to pay some bills, so she put the bite on me just after I was paid my salary.*

PUT THE **CART*** BEFORE THE HORSE
PUT THE **HEAT*** (SCREWS) ON

PUT SOMEONE THROUGH THE WRINGER
to cause great distress, usually with questioning and scolding
[causar mucha angustia, generalmente con interrogatorios y regaños]
> *I was stopped at Customs because I had brought fruit into the country. They put me through the wringer before they let me go.*

PUT TWO AND TWO TOGETHER
to solve a problem with the information that is available
[resolver un problema haciendo inferencias]
> *Jane put two and two together and concluded that Harry was never going to marry her .*

PUT UP A GOOD **FRONT***
PUT UP WITH
to tolerate
[tolerar a]
> *I can put up with Emily as long as she does not shout.*

Q
MIND* ONE'S P'S AND Q'S

ON* THE Q.T.

QUEER
QUEER **DUCK***

QUESTION
BE OUT OF THE QUESTION
not to be considered
[no ser para considerarse]
> *Because of the increase in cholera in Bangladesh, tourist travel there is out of the question.*

POP* THE QUESTION

$64 DOLLAR QUESTION
the most difficult question
[la pregunta de mayor dificultad]
> *How to eliminate unemployment is the 64 dollar question.*

QUITS
CALL* IT QUITS

RACE

RAT RACE

competitive, frenzied, ongoing activity

[actividad constante, competitiva y frenética]

Some of my friends have moved out to the quiet countryside because they dislike the rat-race in the city.

RAGGED

RUN SOMEONE RAGGED

to tire, to give someone too many responsibilties

[cansarle a uno]

My employer ran me ragged from the moment I walked in. No sooner had I finished one job when he gave me another.

RAIN

RAIN **CATS*** AND DOGS

RAINED

BE RAINED OUT

to be cancelled because of bad weather

[ser cancelado a causa del mal tiempo]

Our July 4 picnic was rained out; perhaps we can postpone it for one week.

RAISE

RAISE A **STINK***

RAISE **CAIN***

RAISE **EYEBROWS***

RAKE

HAUL (RAKE) OVER THE **COALS***

RAKE IT IN

to earn a lot of money

[ganar mucho dinero]

Joe thinks that if he bets on his favorite horse, he will rake it in. I think he will probably lose all his money.

RAP

BEAT*** THE RAP

RAT

RAT **RACE***

SMELL A RAT

to suspect something

[sospechar algo]

I smell a rat. A 15% guaranteed return on my investment sounds too good.

RAW

RAW **DEAL***

READ

READ BETWEEN THE **LINES***

READ THE RIOT **ACT***

REAL

ACT* REAL

THE REAL **MCCOY***

REASON

IT STANDS TO REASON. (Usually present tense)

It is logical.

[Es lógico.]

It stands to reason that Emma and Lulu will vacation together; they are good friends.

WITHIN REASON

appropriate, reasonable

[conveniente]

The price he quoted for building the cabinet is within reason.

*Look under the **key word*** for this idiom.

RECORD

OFF THE RECORD

unofficial, confidential

[confidencial]

The journalist promised that anything told to him that day would be off the record.

_____

RED

CATCH SOMEONE RED-HANDED

to find someone in the act of doing something wrong

[encontrar a alguien con las manos en la masa]

The farmer caught two teenagers red-handed stealing a bushel of apples.

_____

IN THE RED

in debt

[con deudas]

Jan is always in the red; she spends more than she earns.

_____

PAINT* THE TOWN RED
RED LETTER DAY*

RED-HANDED

TO CATCH SOMEONE RED*-HANDED

RIDE

LET* IT RIDE

TAKE SOMEONE FOR A RIDE

(1) to cheat someone

[engañar a alguien]

Henry took Bill for a ride; he sold him a piece of someone else's land.

_____

(2) to kill someone

[matar a alguien]

Joe was a gangster. When he was 25 years old, he was taken for a ride. He was never found again.

_____

RIGHT

IN ONE'S RIGHT MIND*
ONE'S HEART* IS IN THE RIGHT PLACE
RIGHT-HAND* MAN
RIGHT OFF THE BAT*
RIGHT UNDER ONE'S NOSE*
SERVE* SOMEONE RIGHT

RILEY

LIVE THE LIFE* OF RILEY

RING

RING A BELL*

RIOT

READ THE RIOT ACT*

RIP

(1) RIP OFF

to cheat or steal

[engañar o robar a]

The dealer ripped me off when I bought new tires for my car. The tires had defects.

_____

(2) RIP-OFF

a situation in which cheating is involved

[un engao]

The price of that TV set is too high. That is a rip-off. You can buy it for half the price at a discount store.

_____

RISE

GET* A RISE OUT OF (SOMEONE)

RISK

RUN (TAKE) A RISK

take a chance; to try something that may not succeed

[tratar de hacer algo que tiene la posibilidad de fracasar]

Sal is very timid. He never takes a risk.

_____

RIVER

SELL SOMEONE DOWN THE RIVER

to betray someone for personal gain

[traiciónar a alguien para sacar una ventaja personal]

Heinz sold Herman down the river when he told the boss that Herman had a criminal record.

UP THE RIVER
 in jail
 [encarcelado]
  Susie has not seen her father since he went up the river. She does not know it is a prison.

ROAD
 LET'S **GET*** THE SHOW ON THE ROAD
 HIT* THE ROAD
 ONE FOR THE ROAD
  one more drink of an alcoholic beverage before leaving
  [una bebida alcohólica más, antes de irse uno]
   Ian was told not to drink and drive, but he had one for he road before he left the party; he crashed into a tree and is now in the hospital.

 ROAD HOG
  a driver who does not permit others to pass easily
  [el que maneja un coche sin darles a los otros la posibilidad de pasar con facilidad]
   The road was narrow. A road hog was driving very slowly, and refused to move aside for the cars behind him to pass.

ROB
 ROB PETER TO PAY **PAUL***
ROBINSON
 BEFORE YOU **CAN*** SAY JACK ROBINSON
ROCK
 BETWEEN A ROCK AND A **HARD*** PLACE
 ROCK THE **BOAT***

ROCKER
 OFF ONE'S ROCKER
  insane
  [loco]
   He is off his rocker if he thinks I'm going to finish this job before the end of the day. This job will take at least three days.

ROCKS
 ON THE ROCKS
  (1) with ice cubes
  [con hielo (en una bebida)]
   He likes his whiskey on the rocks. He thinks the ice improves the taste.
  (2) a failure
  [un fracaso]
   His business is on the rocks. He will lose most of his savings.

ROGER
 ROGER!
  (1) OK. I understand you.
  [Bien. Te (Le(s)) entiendo]
   You want me to stand in front of you on line. Roger!

  (2) When two persons converse on a radio, "Roger!" indicates that one person has finished and the other may begin to speak.
  [Cuando dos personas se comunican por radio, "Roger!" significa que una de las personas ha terminado de hablar y la otra puede comenzar.]
   I hear you clearly. Roger! I will call you tomorrow at the same time. Roger!

ROLLING
 START THE **BALL*** ROLLING
 KEEP THE **BALL*** ROLLING

ROOF
 HIT THE ROOF (**CEILING***)

ROOM
 ELBOW*-ROOM

ROOST
 RULE* THE ROOST

ROOT
 ROOT FOR SOMEONE OR SOMETHING

*Look under the **key word*** for this idiom.

to encourage and cheer for someone or a group to succeed

[animar a alguien o a un grupo con aplausos para que tengan éxito]

I root for the Yankees every time they play.

ROPE
COME* TO THE END OF ONE'S ROPE

ROPE SOMEONE INTO

to force someone to do something

[obligarle a alguien que haga algo]

He roped me into buying ten tickets to his charity benefit.

ROPES
LEARN* THE ROPES

KNOW* THE ROPES

ROSES
NO **BED*** OF ROSES

R.S.V.P.
R.S.V.P.

Please answer (in French, Repondez s'il vous plait.)

[favor de responder (francés)]

The wedding invitations called for me to R.S.V.P.

RUB
RUB OUT

to kill

[matar]

The chief of that gang was rubbed out last night. His body was found in the morning.

RUB SOMEONE THE WRONG WAY

to irritate someone

[molestarle a alguien]

Joan and I will never be friends. She rubs me the wrong way because she is so selfish.

RUB SOMETHING IN

(1) to place a coating of oil, ointment or stain on a surface

[untar una superficie con una capa de aceite, unguento o tinte]

Be sure to rub in the skin lotion when you go out in the sun.

(2) to remind someone repeatedly of some unpleasant experience or failure

[acordarle a alguien constantemente de una experiencia mala o de un fracaso]

Stop rubbing it in that I failed the math test!

RUBBERNECK
RUBBERNECK

to look at the scene of an accident while driving slowly by, thereby causing traffic to be very slow

[curiosear los chóferes de coches al pasar el sitio de un accidente]

The traffic jam was caused by rubbernecking. People slowed down to see the accident.

RUG
PULL THE RUG OUT FROM UNDER

to undermine someone's plans

[minar los planes de alguien]

Just as John was about to open his new flower shop, the bank pulled the rug out from under him by telling him that his loan was not approved.

RULE
RULE OF **THUMB***

RULE THE **ROOST***

RULE OUT

to eliminate

[eliminar]

The doctor ruled out a heart condition as the reason for Fred's fatigue.

RUN

DRY* RUN

IN THE **LONG*** RUN

RUN **AMUCK***

RUN A **RISK***

RUN ACROSS SOMETHING OR SOMEONE

to encounter

[encontrar]

I ran across Mary at the meat store this morning.

RUN AROUND IN **CIRCLES***

RUNDOWN

a summary

[un resumen]

Give me a rundown of what happened at the meeting last night.

BE RUN DOWN

to be in poor condition

[de malas condicines]

Henry is quite run down as a result of his working long hours at his job.

RUN-OF-THE-**MILL***

RUN OUT OF SOMETHING

to have no more of

[no tener más de]

We've run out of paper towels, and we need them badly.

RUN SOMEONE **RAGGED***

RUNAROUND

GIVE SOMEONE (**GET***) THE RUNAROUND

RUNNING

RUNNING **NOSE***

RUSH

THE **BUM'S*** RUSH

BE IN A RUSH

to be in a hurry

[apresurado]

Mom is always in a rush to get things done. That is why she is able to accomplish so much.

RUT

BE IN A RUT

to be going nowhere, doing the same thing again and again

[sin la esperanza de tener un cambio]

John is in a rut. There is no chance of being promoted to a higher position in his job.

SACK

HIT* THE HAY (SACK)

SAID

EASIER* SAID THAN DONE

SALT

SALT AWAY

to save

[ahorrar]

For the past ten years, John salted away a few dollars each week for his son's college tuition.

SALT OF THE EARTH

a wonderful person

[una persona maravillosa]

My fifth grade teacher was the salt of the earth.

TAKE WITH A **GRAIN*** OF SALT

SAME

IN THE SAME **BOAT***

ON THE SAME **WAVELENGTH***

SAVE

SAVE ONE'S **BREATH***

SAVE **FACE***

*Look under the **key word*** for this idiom.

SAY

BEFORE YOU **CAN*** SAY JACK ROBINSON
SAY A **MOUTHFUL***
SAY (**CRY***) UNCLE
TO SAY **NOTHING*** OF

SAYING

GO* WITHOUT SAYING

SCARCE

MAKE* ONESELF SCARCE

SCARE

SCARE THE **DAYLIGHTS*** OUT OF

SCORE

SETTLE THE SCORE
to avenge oneself
[vengarse]
Tom settled the score with his neighbor by building a high fence that blocked his view.

SCOT

SCOT **FREE***

SCRAPE

SCRAPE THE BOTTOM OF THE **BARREL***

SCRATCH

FROM SCRATCH
from the beginning
[desde el principio]
I baked that cake from scratch. No mixes for me!

SCRATCH THE SURFACE
to begin
[empezar]
I've barely scratched the surface in trying to understand the history of Balkan conflicts.

SCREAM

SCREAM (YELL) **BLOODY*** MURDER

SCREW

HAVE A SCREW LOOSE

to be insane, crazy
[estar chiflado]
Joe acts as though he has a screw loose in his head.

SCREW UP SOMETHING

to make a mess of something
[arruinar]
Instead of repairing it, Jess screwed up the computer. It doesn't even turn on now.

SCREWS

PUT* THE SCREWS (HEAT) ON

SCROUNGE

SCROUNGE AROUND
to hunt in many places
[buscar en muchos lugares]
Nat scrounged around for hours in the basement looking for nuts, bolts and washers for his project.

SEA

BETWEEN THE DEVIL AND THE DEEP **BLUE*** SEA

SEAMS

COME* APART AT THE SEAMS

SEARCH

SEARCH ME! (PRESENT TENSE ONLY!)
I don't know!
[No lo sé.]
You want to know why the moon looks so large on the horizon? Search me! No one knows the answer.

SEAT

BACK* SEAT DRIVER
HOT* SEAT
ON THE **EDGE*** OF ONE'S SEAT

SECOND

ON SECOND THOUGHT
> having changed one's mind
> [como cambio de opinion]
>> *On second thought, I will go to the concert with you.*

PLAY SECOND **FIDDLE***

SECONDHAND
> used, previously owned
> [de segunda mano]
>> *Secondhand clothes are economical. Using them helps prevent waste on this planet.*

TO SECOND **GUESS***

SEE

SEE **DAYLIGHT***

SEE **EYE*** TO EYE

SEE SOMEONE OFF
> to say farewell to someone at the starting point of a journey
> [acompañar a alguien hasta el lugar de embarque para un viaje, y decirle adios alli]
>> *When our friends went to the west coast, we saw them off at the airport.*

SEE THROUGH SOMEONE
> to perceive the truth, in spite of the fact that someone is trying to deceive
> [comprender a pesar de que alguien trata de decepciónar]
>> *Roger saw through the salesman's description of the advantages of living next to the runway of the airport.*

SEE SOMETHING THROUGH
> to conclude a project
> [concluir un proyecto]
>> *When her mother had to leave in the middle of the paint job, Hilda promised that she would see it through.*

SELL

SELL DOWN THE **RIVER***

SELL LIKE **HOTCAKES***
> to be sold rapidly
> [venderse y agotarse algo rápidamente]
>> *The imported gloves sold like hotcakes. They were well made and inexpensive.*

SELL ONESELF SHORT
> to undervalue oneself
> [menospreciarse; darse de menos]
>> *You are a very good worker. Don't sell yourself short.*

SELL OUT
> (1) to sell ownership in a business (part or full)
> [vennder alguien su propiedad en un negocio]
>> *I sold out my shares in the pizza shop. The price was good and I needed the money.*

> (2) to betray
> [traicionar]
>> *In order to save himself, the thief sold out his partner to the police.*

> (3) to have every seat at a performance sold
> [tener vendidos todos los asientos en una función]
>> *Saturday's performance at the opera sold out two weeks in advance.*

SELL SOMEONE A **BILL*** OF GOODS

SEND

SEND SOMEONE INTO **ORBIT*** (TO THE MOON)

SEND SOMEONE **PACKING***

SENSE
HORSE* SENSE

SERVE
SERVE ONE'S **PURPOSE***

SERVE SOMEONE RIGHT
to deserve the punishment one has received
[merecer uno el castigo que ha recibido]
> *It served Nat right to have to eat alone after being so rude to his friends and family.*

_____

SERVE TIME (DO TIME)
to spend time in prison
[pasar algún tiempo en la cárcel]
> *Al served time in Sing Sing for assault and robbery.*

_____

SET
HAVE ONE'S **HEART*** SET ON
SET **FIRE*** TO

SET OUT
to start
[comenzar]
> *We set out on our trip at 8 in the morning.*

_____

SET SOMEONE BACK
to cost a lot
[costar]
> *This jacket set me back $150.*

_____

SET SOMEONE UP WITH SOMEONE
(1) to put someone in contact with
[poner a alguien en contacto con]
> *We set Mary up with Jim hoping that they would like and see more of each other.*

_____

TO SET SOMEONE UP
(2) to put someone is a position that is harmful
[meter a alguien en una situación peligrosa]
> *The gang chief arranged for Al to be set up as the person to be arrested for pushing drugs.*

_____

SETTLE
SETTLE THE **SCORE***

SEVENTH
IN SEVENTH **HEAVEN***

SHAKE
SHAKE A **LEG***

SHAKE IT UP
to hurry, to move quickly
[darse prisa]
> *Elsie is always late for the school bus. I asked her to please shake it up.*

_____

SHAKE UP
a reorganization
[una reorganización]
> *After the investigation, there was a shake up at the bank, and the head teller was fired.*

_____

SHAKY
ON SHAKY **GROUND***

SHAPE
BE OUT OF SHAPE
to be in poor physical condition
[estar de malas condiciónes físicas]
> *Jed has not been well for some time, so he is out of shape.*

_____

SHAPE UP
to develop (referring to a person or a project)
[desarrollar]
> *How is the book you're writing shaping up?*

SHAPE-UP

a place (sometimes a street corner) where people seeking employment for the day gather in the morning, and where people seeking help come to hire day-laborers

[un lugar (a veces la esquina de una calle) donde la gente que busca empleo para ese día se congrega por la mañana, y donde la gente quien busca trabajadores acuden a emplear jornaleros]

Joe was a dock worker. Every morning he went to the shape-up with all the other men, hoping to get a job for the day.

SHARE

THE **LION'S*** SHARE

SHAVE

CLOSE* SHAVE

SHEEP

BLACK* SHEEP

SHEEP'S

WOLF IN SHEEP'S **CLOTHING***

SHELL

SHELL OUT

to pay, to spend

[pagar]

I had to shell out two dollars for that pencil!

SHINE

TAKE A SHINE TO

to become fond of

[hacerse amigo de]

Mattie took a shine to Laurie the first time he met her.

SHIP

SHIP OUT

to leave port on a ship

[enviar]

After two weeks of practice in the Japanese language, Tom shipped out to Japan.

SHIPSHAPE

in good order

[en orden]

Finally Timmie tidied up his toys and now they are in shipshape order.

SHIRT

LOSE* ONE'S SHIRT

STUFFED SHIRT

someone who is pompous

[un tragavirotes]

Mr. Castle is just a stuffed shirt. He cannot tolerate anyone at the the office calling him by his first name.

SHOES

IN SOMEONE'S SHOES

in someone else's position or place

[en las circunstancias de otra persona]

A limousine delivers and picks up Ron at work every day. I wish I were in his shoes.

SHOESTRING

ON A SHOESTRING

with very little money

[con muy poco dinero]

Long ago Mr. Sears started his business on a shoestring, and now it is a big and successful-company.

SHOOK

SHOOK SOMEONE UP

upset

*Look under the **key word*** for this idiom.

[desconcertado]

Although I was not injured, the train accident shook me up.

SHOOT

SHOOT FROM THE **HIP***

SHOOT FULL OF **HOLES***

SHOOT OFF ONE'S **MOUTH***

SHOOT ONE'S WAD

to spend all of one's money

[gastar uno todo su dinero]

Van shot his wad on the engagement ring for Diane.

SHOOT THE **BREEZE***

SHOP

BULL* IN A CHINA SHOP

SHOP AROUND

(1) to compare prices of products or services in different places

[comparar los precios en varios lugares]

I shopped around for a computer, but I found the best price in a place near home.

(2) to make comparisons of different authorities or persons

[comparar a distintas autoridades o personas]

Mrs. Steen shopped around until she found a doctor who was willing to prescribe sleeping pills for her.

SWEATSHOP

a factory that has very poor working conditions and very low pay

[una fábrica de condiciónes pésimas para los trabajadores y de salarios muy bajos]

Kathy could not feed herself on what she earned in that sweatshop. Furthermore, the poor light was ruining her eyes.

TALK SHOP

to talk about one's work

[hablar uno sobre su trabajo]

Cary doesn't enjoy visiting that group of teachers. They spend all their time talking shop even when they are not in school.

SHORT

CAUGHT* SHORT

SELL* ONESELF SHORT

SHORT **END*** OF THE STICK

TO BE SHORTHANDED

to have less help than is needed to do the work

[tener menos ayudantes en el trabajo de los que son necesarios]

The office is shorthanded because two of the secretaries have the flu.

SHOT

BIG* SHOT

GIVE IT ONE'S **BEST*** SHOT

HOT* SHOT

SHOTS

CALL* THE SHOTS

SHOULDER

CHIP* ON ONE'S SHOULDER

COLD* SHOULDER

HAVE A GOOD **HEAD*** ON ONE'S SHOULDERS

STRAIGHT FROM THE SHOULDER

frankly

[francamente]

Let me tell you straight from the shoulder that I don't like the way you are treating your husband.

SHOULDERS

ON ONE'S SHOULDERS

burdened

[cargado de penas]

Martha is always worried. She carries everyone's troubles on her shoulders.

SHOW
LET'S **GET*** THE SHOW ON THE ROAD.

SHOW-OFF
someone who tries to attract attention with behavior or appearance

[alguien que trata de llamar la atención de los demás con su comportamiento o su apariencia]

She is not a show-off. She is quiet, her clothing is simple, and she is actually shy.

SHOW UP
to arrive

[llegar]

She showed up just in time for the movie.

TO SHOW SOMEONE UP
to surpass in skill or performance

[exponer los fracasos de otra persona]

I lifted the 100 pound weight with two hands. John showed me up by lifting the same weight with one hand.

SHRUG

SHRUG OFF SOMETHING OR SOMEONE
to pay no attention to

[no hacerle caso a]

Lois shrugged off not being promoted on the job; she intended to leave the job anyway.

SHUT
OPEN* AND SHUT CASE

SICK

SICK AND TIRED
to be annoyed

[fastidiado]

I am sick and tired of having to pick up after you.

SIDE
GET UP ON THE WRONG SIDE OF THE **BED***

SIDE WITH
to align oneself with

[aliarse con]

I side with Mae in this dispute.

SIDE-SWIPE
for the side of one car to collide with the side of another car

[chocar el lado de un coche con el lado de otro]

He sideswiped my car on the right side, while it was parked at the curb.

WRONG SIDE OF THE **TRACKS***

SIGHT

KNOW A PERSON BY SIGHT
to recognize a person

[reconocer a una persona sin saber su nombre]

Don't describe Ella to me. I'll find her. I know her by sight.

SIGN

SIGN OFF
to end transmitting on the radio, television or telephone

[terminar una transmisión de radio, televisión, o una llamada telefónica]

I'm signing off now. I am finished.

TO SIGN OFF ON SOMETHING
to sign a document, permitting it to go to the next step

[firmar un documento]

I read the mortgage agreement, and signed off on it. It can go to the bank now.

*Look under the **key word*** for this idiom.

SILLY

TICKLED SILLY (PINK*)

SIMMER

SIMMER DOWN

to become calm

[calmarse]

> *It took Mary two hours to simmer down after her quarrel with Andy.*

_____

SINK

SINK ONE'S TEETH INTO

(1) to bite into

[morder]

> *I couldn't wait to sink my teeth into that watermelon.*

(2) to devote oneself to working on something

[dedicarse a trabajar en algo]

> *Reva sank her teeth into learning how to sew zippers into clothes.*

_____

SINK OR SWIM

doing something, not knowing whether one will fail or succeed

[haciendo algo sin saber si uno va a fracasar o tener éxito]

> *I decided to risk going into business with Patty, sink or swim.*

_____

SINKER

HOOK*, LINE AND SINKER

SIT

SIT THERE LIKE A **BUMP*** ON A LOG

SIT IN ON

to observe

[observar]

> *I sat in on the rehearsal for GUYS AND DOLLS, and enjoyed it immensely.*

_____

SIT ON THE **FENCE***

SIT TIGHT

to wait

[esperar]

> *The line for the ferry was very long, but the man at the gate suggested that we sit tight, and we'd probably get on.*

_____

SITTING

SITTING **PRETTY***

SIX

SIX **FEET*** UNDER

SIXTY-FOUR DOLLAR

SIXTY-FOUR DOLLAR **QUESTION***

SIZE

CUT* SOMEONE DOWN TO SIZE

SIZE UP SOMEONE OR SOMETHING

to appraise

[apreciar]

> *Sam sized up the interviewer correctly, and answered his questions cleverly. He was hired for the job. At the same time, the interviewer sized him up.*

_____

SKATE

SKATE ON THIN **ICE***

SKELETON

SKELETON IN THE **CLOSET***

SKIDS

HIT* THE SKIDS

SKIN

BY THE SKIN OF ONE'S TEETH

succeeding, but almost failing

[a duras penas]

> *Rebecca passed the examination with a grade of 60; this was the lowest passing grade. She passed by the skin of her teeth.*

_____

GET* UNDER SOMEONE'S SKIN

SKY

PIE* IN THE SKY

SLEEP

SLEEP LIKE A TOP

to sleep soundly, very well

[dormir a pierna suelta]

I am completely rested; last night I slept like a top.

_____

SLEEP ON IT

to postpone making a decision, usually until the next day.

[consultar con la almohada]

Pam decide to sleep on which automobile to buy.

_____

SLEEVE

HAVE SOMETHING UP ONE'S SLEEVE

to have a secret plan

[tener un motivo secreto]

Dan had something up his sleeve when he proposed that the class should go birdwatching instead of to the zoo. He lived next to the bird sanctuary.

_____

LAUGH* UP ONE'S SLEEVE

SLIDE

LET* SOMETHING SLIDE

SLING

SLING HASH*

SLIP

PINK* SLIP

SLIP OF THE TONGUE

something said that the speaker did not mean to say

[algo que alguien dice sin querer]

Mary made a slip of the tongue when she told Sarah that she was going to the wedding

_____

SLIP ONE'S MIND*

SLIP THROUGH ONE'S FINGERS*

SMART

GET* SMART

SMELL

SMELL A RAT*

SMELL SOMETHING FISHY*

SMOKE

GO* UP IN SMOKE

SMOKER

CHAIN* SMOKER

SMOOTH

SMOOTH OVER A PROBLEM

to resolve a problem peacefully

[resolver un problema con calma]

Mama tried to smooth over the disagreement between Mary and John.

_____

SNAP

A SNAP

to be very easy

[algo fácil]

Repairing that chair is a snap for Martin.

_____

SNAP OUT OF IT

to suddenly improve one's emotional or physical state

[mejorar uno su estado emocional o fisico subitamente]

Mary was depressed after losing her job; finally she snapped out of it.

_____

SNAPPY

MAKE IT SNAPPY! (USUALLY PRESENT TENSE)

Hurry! Do it quickly!

[¡Rápido!]

Make it snappy. The train leaves in five minutes.

_____

113

*Look under the **key word*** for this idiom.

SNEEZE

NOTHING TO SNEEZE AT

something to take notice of

[algo de importancia]

He offered me $1700 for my old car. That is nothing to sneeze at.

SNOW

GIVE* SOMEONE A SNOW JOB

SNOWBALL'S

SNOWBALL'S CHANCE* IN HELL

SOAP

SOFT SOAP SOMEONE

to flatter

[halagar]

Please don't soft soap me. Flattery won't get you anywhere.

SOB

SOB STORY

a story that is intended to gain sympathy

[una historia contada para ganarle a uno su compasión]

He told me his sob story about his terrible childhood, and how difficult it was for him to make friends.

SOCK

SOCK IT TO SOMEONE

to speak strongly and clearly to a person

[hablarle a una persona con claridad y fuerza]

The football coach really socked it to the team: he told them that if they lost the next game, it would mean the end of football at the school.

SOFT

SOFT SOAP*

SOFT TOUCH

someone from whom one can borrow easily

[alguien a quien es facil pedir cosas prestadas]

Lenny lent me the $100 I needed. He is such a soft touch.

SONG

FOR A SONG

inexpensively

[por poco dinero]

I bought this leather jacket for a song.

SONG AND DANCE*

SWAN SONG

someone's last performance, or work

[la última obra de un artista]

Even though Judy Garland's swan song was many years ago, we are lucky that TV has captured her performances for us, and we can still hear her sing.

SORE

SORE LOSER*

SORROWS

DROWN* ONE'S SORROWS

SORTS

OUT OF SORTS

(1) in a bad mood

[de mal humor]

Stay away from her. She is out of sorts and will get angry for no reason at all.

(2) not feeling well
[algo mal de salud]
I have a slight headache; I'm a bit out of sorts.
I'll lie down for a while.

_____

SOUND

SOUND OFF
to give one's opinion loudly
[dar uno su opinion a voces]
Jack sounded off on how unfair he thought the
test had been.

_____

SOUR

SOUR **GRAPES***

SPACE

SPACE CADET
one who is distracted, preoccupied
[una persona constantemente distraída]
Don't expect to get an intelligent answer to your
questions about mother from Bob. He is a
space cadet.

_____

SPACED

SPACED OUT
dreamy, inattentive
[distraído]
It's hard to get Adam's attention; he looks half-
asleep. He is really spaced out.

_____

SPEAK

SPEAK WITH **FORKED*** TONGUE

SPICK-AND-SPAN

SPICK-AND-SPAN
neat and clean
[pulcro y limpio]
The house was spick-and-span when we left
it, and I hope it stays that way for a while.

_____

SPILL

SPILL THE **BEANS***

SPIN

SPIN A TALE (THE WORD **TALE** MAY BE MODIFIED.)
to tell a story
[contar una historia]
Jesse could spin one tale after another all night
without a rest. We all loved to listen.

_____

SPIN ONE'S WHEELS
to be exerting energy uselessly
[echar fuerzas, pero sin éxito]
The car spun its wheels in the ice, but we could
not get it out of the rut.

_____

SPINE-CHILLING

SPINE-CHILLING
frightening
[escalofriante]
The newspaper reports of accidental killings
by guns are spine-chilling.

_____

SPITTING

SPITTING **IMAGE***

SPLIT

SPLIT **HAIRS***
SPLIT UP
to separate
[separarse]
Don and Marie have decided to split up. After
six years of marriage, they will separate.

_____

SPONGE

THROW IN THE SPONGE (TOWEL)
to admit defeat; to give up, surrender
[darse por vencido]
By the time the wrestler threw in the sponge,
he had two swollen eyes, and a dozen bad
bruises.

*Look under the **key word*** for this idiom.

SPOON

GREASY* SPOON

SPORT

GOOD* SPORT

SPOT

HIT* THE SPOT

ON THE SPOT

(1) in the right place

[en el lugar correcto]

I was on the spot when Mary fell, and so I was able to help her.

(2) in a difficult situation

[en una situación difícil]

When they found the missing key in Tom's pocket, he was on the spot.

SPREAD

SPREAD (POUR*, PUT, LAY) IT ON THICK

SPRUCE

SPRUCE UP

to freshen up, to improve the appearance of someone or something

[asear, asearse]

Let me spruce up before we go out to dinner.

SQUARE

FAIR* AND SQUARE

SQUARE ONE

the beginning

[el principio]

Let me start at the beginning in building this model airplane. I like to start from square one.

SQUAWK

BELLYACHE (BEEF*, GRIPE, SQUAWK, KICK)

SQUEAL

SQUEAL ON SOMEONE

to inform on someone, to report someone to an authority

[denunciar a alguien]

The police arrested three suspects for stealing the car. They found them because one of their friends squealed on them.

SQUEEZE

TIGHT SQUEEZE

a difficult situation

[una situación difícil]

Ross is in a tight squeeze. He has high medical bills from a long illness. If he pays the doctor, he can't pay the rent.

STAB

STAB SOMEONE IN THE BACK

to betray someone

[traiciónar a alguien]

Zev stabbed me in the back by telling the boss that I am an alcoholic. They refused to hire me.

STACK

BLOW* ONE'S STACK

STAKES

PULL* UP STAKES

STAND

A LEG* TO STAND ON

MAKE ONE'S HAIR STAND ON END*

STAND A CHANCE

to have a possibility

[tener la posibilidad]

I don't stand a chance of winning the tennis cup.

STAND FOR

to represent

[representar]

Many people come to this country because they feel that it stands for freedom.

___

STAND ON ONE'S OWN TWO FEET*

STAND OUT

to be noticeable

[sobresalir]

Minnie's red hair stands out in a crowd. You can find her instantly.

___

STAND SOMEONE UP

to fail to keep an appointment with someone

[no presentarse en una cita con alguien]

Larry stood Mary up Saturday night when they had a date to go to the movies.

___

STAND TO REASON*

STAND UP FOR

to defend

[proteger]

Joan stands up for her rights at all times. She doesn't let anyone take advantage of her.

___

STAND UP TO SOMEONE

to resist someone

[resistir a alguien]

When the older boys stopped Jim and asked him for a quarter, he stood up to them, and refused.

___

STANDS

IT STANDS TO **REASON***

START

START OFF ON THE WRONG **FOOT***

START THE **BALL*** ROLLING

STEADY

GOING* STEADY

STEAL

BE A STEAL

be a bargain

[ser una ganga]

The price for that cashmere coat is so low that it's a steal.

___

STEAL SOMEONE'S THUNDER

to say in advance what someone else intended to say

[ser el primero en decir lo que quería otra persona decir]

He stole my thunder by telling my funniest joke before I did.

___

STEAM

BLOW* OFF STEAM

LET OFF STEAM (SEE **BLOW***)

STEAMED

GET* STEAMED UP

STEER

STEER **CLEAR*** OF SOMEONE

STEP

STEP ON THE GAS! STEP ON IT!

Hurry! Do it quickly!

[¡Rapido!]

We should have left five minutes ago, and you're not even dressed yet. Step on the gas! Step on it!

___

STEP (**GET***) OUT OF LINE

STEVEN

EVEN*-STEVEN

STICK

SHORT **END*** OF THE STICK

STICK AROUND

to remain

[quedarse]

117

I stuck around after the party, hoping that they would invite me to the next party that they were planning.

_____

STICK ONE'S **NECK*** OUT

STICK ONE'S **NOSE*** INTO

STICK OUT
   to be noticeable
   [sobresalir]
   Dan is so tall he sticks out in a crowd of children.

_____

STICK SOMEONE WITH
   to burden someone with
   [echarle a alguien la responsabilidad de]
   They tried to stick me with the whole cleanup operation.

_____

STICK TO ONE'S **GUNS***

STICK UP FOR
   to defend, protect
   [defender]
   Josie sticks up for her little sister Susie when people make fun of her.

_____

STICK WITH IT; STICK IT OUT
   to be persistent
   [ser persistente]
   I admire Andy; he doesn't give up. He sticks with it until he finds a solution.

_____

STICKY
HAVE STICKY **FINGERS***

STIFF
KEEP A STIFF UPPER **LIP***

STINK
RAISE A STINK
   to make a fuss

[armar un jaleo]
   Mom will raise a stink when she finds out that you ate all the chicken that she was planning to use for supper.

_____

STIR
STIR SOMEONE UP; STIR UP SOMEONE
   to get someone excited
   [agitar a alguien]
   Everything was peaceful and quiet until Tom stirred us up with stories about muggers.

_____

STITCHES
IN STITCHES
   in uncontrollable laughter
   [con risa loca]
   The Laurel and Hardy comedies kept us in stitches.

_____

STOCK
LOCK, STOCK AND **BARREL***

STOMACH
TURN SOMEONE'S STOMACH
   to make someone feel nauseous
   [dar asco a alguien]
   The sight of that accident turned my stomach.

_____

STONE
KILL TWO **BIRDS*** WITH ONE STONE

STONED
BE STONED
   to be drunk or drugged
   [borracho o drogado]
   After smoking marajuana, she was so stoned she could barely walk.

_____

STOP
STOP **BUGGING*** SOMEONE
PIT* STOP

STOPS
THE **BUCK*** STOPS HERE

STORE
MIND* THE STORE

STORY
COCK AND **BULL*** STORY

SOB* STORY

STRAIGHT
GIVE* IT TO SOMEONE STRAIGHT
GO* STRAIGHT
STRAIGHT FROM THE **HORSE***'S MOUTH
STRAIGHT FROM THE **SHOULDER***

STRAPPED
BE STRAPPED FOR MONEY
to be with little or no money
[con poco dinero o ninguno]
Jules was so strapped for money that he could not buy a subway token.

STRAW
LAST* STRAW

STREET
ON **EASY*** STREET

STRETCH
STRETCH A **POINT***

STRIKE
STRIKE OUT
(1) to start something new
[iniciar algo]
Josie loved to sew, so she decided to strike out as a costume mistress in the theatre.

(2) to fail to hit the baseball three times at the home plate
[no golpear la pelota tres veces (beísbol)]
Bill was not playing his best. He struck out three times during the game.

STRIKE WHILE THE IRON IS **HOT***

STRIKES
HAVE TWO STRIKES AGAINST ONE
to have two disadvantages
[tener dos desventajas en contra]
Mary has two strikes against her when she applies for the bookkeeping job: she can't do math and she is afraid of the computer.

STRING
STRING SOMEONE ALONG
to keep someone interested or friendly, without feeling sincerely about that person
[tener a alguien engañado]
Leslie strung Tim along. When she had no other dates, she went out with him, pretending that she liked him.

STRINGS
STRINGS **ATTACHED***
PULL STRINGS
to use influence and personal acquaintances to get something done
[mover palancas]
Joey pulled strings to get the job at the bank. He knew the bank manager.

STUCK
TO BE STUCK UP
to feel superior, to be a snob
[ser un estirado]
I feel very uncomfortable with Herb; he is so stuck up.

STUFFED
STUFFED **SHIRT***

*Look under the **key word*** for this idiom.

SUIT

BIRTHDAY* SUIT

SUIT YOURSELF

do as you please; make your own decision
[¡Haz (Haga(-n))lo que quieras(-a(-n))!]

Please come Monday or Tuesday to mow the lawn; suit yourself.

SUPER

SUPER DUPER

excellent; outstanding
[sobresaliente]

That ice cream cone was super duper.

SURFACE

SCRATCH THE **SURFACE***

SURPRISE

TAKE SOMEONE BY SURPRISE

to surprise someone
[sorprender a alguien]

Connie took me by surprise when she walked into my typing class. I thought she was away on vacation.

SWAN

SWAN **SONG***

SWEAT

SWEAT **BULLETS***

SWEATSHOP

SWEAT**SHOP***

SWELL

A SWELL

a dandy; one who wears fancy clothes and shows off
[una pesona elegante]

The fellow at that table is a swell. He must spend a fortune on his clothes, and he loves to show it.

SWELL

very good

[muy bueno]

That ice cream sundae was swell.

SWIM

SINK* OR SWIM

SWING

SWING SOMETHING

to make something happen that is difficult
[realizar algo difícil]

Jerry just swung a deal to sell his house. He will get enough money to retire.

GET* IN THE SWING OF THINGS

𝒯-𝒰-𝒱-𝒲-𝒳-𝒴-𝒵

TAB

PICK UP THE TAB

to pay the bill, usually in a restaurant or a bar
[pagar la cuenta (generalmente en un restaurante o un bar)]

Dad usually picks up the tab when we go out to dinner.

TABLE

LAY (PUT) ONE'S CARDS* ON THE TABLE

TURN THE TABLES ON SOMEONE

to change almost certain defeat into victory over someone
[convertir una derrota por alguien en una victoria]

By a brilliant move, Sergei escaped from a trap in chess, and trapped his opponent. He turned the tables on his opponent.

UNDER THE TABLE

secretly
[a escondidas]

The janitor was not supposed to accept gifts from the tenants. However, the tenants paid him under the table for prompt service.

TACKS

GET DOWN TO BRASS* TACKS

TAKE

TAKE A BEATING*
TAKE A CRACK* AT
TAKE A GANDER* AT
TAKE A POWDER*
TAKE (RUN) A RISK*
TAKE A SEAT*
TAKE A SHINE* TO
TAKE AFTER SOMEONE

to resemble
[parecer a, imitar a]

Rosie takes after her mother; she looks just like her.

TAKE CHARGE*
TAKE INTO ACCOUNT*
TAKE IT EASY*
TAKE OFF

(1) to become successful
[tener éxito]

Gerald set up shop selling the kite that he invented, and the business has suddenly taken off.

(2) to begin an airplane flight
[tener exito]

That plane took off one hour late.

(3) to leave
[tener exito]

He took off in a hurry.

TAKE-OFF

a parody
[una parodia]

When Alice sang OVER THE RAINBOW, it was a perfect take-off on Judy Garland.

TAKE ON

to accept responsibility; to assume a burden
[emprender]

I agreed that I would take on the extra job of baby sitting on weekends while the regular babysitter was on vacation.

*Look under the **key word*** for this idiom.

TAKE ONE'S **HAT** OFF TO SOMEONE

TAKE ONE'S TIME

to do something slowly

[hacer algo lentamente[

I like to take my time when I cook from a new recipe.

_____

TAKE-OUT

food brought home from a restaurant

[comida entregada a casa de un restaurante]

Tonight let's have a take-out from the pizza place on the corner.

_____

TAKE OVER SOMEONE OR SOMETHING; TAKE SOMETHING OVER

to assume control of

[controlar]

Jim will take the selling job over on the first of next month.

_____

TAKE **PAINS***

TAKE **PART*** IN

TAKE **PITY*** ON

TAKE SOMEONE AT HIS/HER **WORD***

TAKE SOMEONE BY **SURPRISE***   TAKE SOMEONE FOR **SOMEONE ELSE**

to mistake one person for another

[confundir a dos personas]

I was embarrassed because I took Tommy for Henry; they are the same height and both have dark hair.

_____

TAKE SOMEONE FOR A **RIDE***

TAKE SOMEONE OUT; TAKE OUT SOMEONE

(1) to remove someone or something

[sacar a alguien o algo]

The baseball coach decided to take out the pitcher because he was doing so poorly in the game.

_____

(2) to take someone on a date

[salir con alguien]

Jim is looking forward to taking Mary out next Saturday night.

_____

TAKE (SOMEONE) TO THE **CLEANERS***

TAKE SOMETHING FOR **GRANTED***

TAKE SOMETHING **LYING*** DOWN

TAKE SOMETHING TO **HEART***

TAKE SOMETHING UP WITH SOMEONE

to discuss something with someone

[conferir con alguien sobre algo]

I decided to take up with my mother the problem of taking Nancy to school every day. I need some relief from that errand.

_____

TAKE THE **BULL*** BY THE HORNS

TAKE THE **CAKE***

TAKE THE **FIFTH***

TAKE THE **PLUNGE***

TAKE THE WORDS OUT OF ONE'S **MOUTH***

TAKE TIME OFF

to stop work for a period

[dejar de trabajar por una temporada]

I had to take time off from work when my grandmother came from California to visit me.

_____

TAKE TURNS

to alternate doing something with someone else

[alternar]

We took turns dealing the cards when we played Casino.

_____

TAKE WITH A **GRAIN*** OF SALT

TAKEN

GET* TAKEN

TAKES

HAVE WHAT IT TAKES

to have the skills and/or personality to be successful

[tener las habilidades o la personalidad para tener éxito]

Anne has what it takes as a real estate salesperson.

_____

SPIN* A TALE

TALL TALE

a story that could not be true

[una historia inverosímil]

Ellen told a tall tale about why she was late to school. She said her alarm clock had started going backwards!

_____

TALK

PEP* TALK

TALK **BACK***

TALK **SHOP***

TALK TO THE WALL

to try to communicate with someone who does not listen

[hablar uno con alguien que no le hace caso]

Dan is frustrated because when he asks John for help he feels as though he were talking to the wall.

_____

TALK THROUGH ONE'S HAT

to talk nonsense

[decir disparates]

The city tour guide talked through his hat when he described the famous buildings and their history. He was all wrong.

_____

TALK TURKEY

to speak frankly and bluntly

[hablar francamente]

The builder came over this afternoon to talk turkey. We went over the building plans, and he told us how much each item would cost.

_____

TALL

TALL TALE*

TASTE

TO GET A TASTE (**DOSE***) OF ONE'S OWN MEDICINE

TAT

TIT FOR TAT

the equal of what was received, usually a hurt

[tal para cual]

Jack poured ink over my notebook, so I did the same to his notebook. That was tit for tat.

_____

TEA

ONE'S **CUP*** OF TEA

TEAPOT

TEMPEST IN A TEAPOT

a big fuss about a small matter

[la exageración de un asunto de poca importancia]

It was a tempest in a teapot when the waiter scolded Diane for dirtying one of the dishes on the newly set table.

_____

TEAR

TEAR INTO SOMEONE

to scold

[reñir a]

Sally tore into me for failing to follow the doctor's orders to rest after my surgery.

_____

TEARJERKER

an overly sentimental story that is intended to make the listener cry

[una historia resentimental contada para hacer llorar al oyente]

We saw a tearjerker movie last night. It was about orphaned children.

_____

TEAR SOMEONE DOWN

to criticize and belittle someone

*Look under the **key word*** for this idiom.

[criticar y despreciar a alguien]
The Russians considered Stalin a hero during his lifetime. He was torn down later because of his crimes.

TEARS
BURST* INTO TEARS
CROCODILE* TEARS

TEETH
BY THE **SKIN*** OF ONE'S TEETH
KICK* IN THE TEETH (PANTS)
SINK* ONE'S TEETH INTO

TELL
TELL **APART***

TELL IT LIKE IT IS
to speak truthfully
[decir la verdad]
Henry will tell me about his life as a soldier. He will tell it like it is.

TELL ONE THING OR PERSON FROM THE OTHER
to distinguish one thing or person from another
[distinguir entre cosas o personas]
The twins look so much alike that I have a lot of trouble telling one from the other.

TELL SOMEONE OFF; TELL SOMEONE A THING OR TWO
to scold someone
[reñir a alguien]
Gilbert told Jones a thing or two when he discovered that he (Jones) had borrowed his car without permission.

TEMPER
LOSE ONE'S TEMPER
to become angry
[enojarse]
I lose my temper too often. I should remain calm.

TEMPEST
TEMPEST IN A **TEAPOT***

TENTERHOOKS
BE ON TENTERHOOKS
to be in suspense
[en ascuas]
James was on tenterhooks, waiting to see if he was accepted at his state university.

THICK
PUT (**POUR***, SPREAD, LAY IT ON) THICK

THROUGH THICK AND THIN
through bad times as well as good
[por los momentos malos y los momentos buenos]
When they got married, they vowed to stay together through thick and thin.

THIN
SKATE ON THIN **ICE***
THROUGH **THICK*** AND THIN

THING
TELL* SOMEONE A THING OR TWO
THINGS
GET* IN THE SWING OF THINGS

THINK
HAVE ANOTHER THINK (**GUESS***) COMING

THINK UP
to have an idea
[inventar]
I just thought up another way of repairing the gas range.

THIRD
THIRD **DEGREE***

THOUGHT

ON **SECOND*** THOUGHT

THOUSAND

BAT* A THOUSAND

THROAT

JUMP DOWN SOMEONE'S THROAT

to react to someone in an aggressive way

[reacciónar a una persona de una manera brava]

He jumped down my throat when I asked where he had been last night. He said it was none of my business.

THROW

THROW **COLD*** WATER ON

THROW A **FIT***

THROW IN THE **SPONGE*** (TOWEL)

THROW ONE'S WEIGHT AROUND

to use one's influence

[mover palancas]

Sam threw his weight around when they planned the party, and so everything was decided according to his wishes.

THROW SOMEONE A **CURVE*** BALL

THROW THE **BOOK*** AT SOMEONE

THROW UP

to vomit

[vomitar]

I had a mild case of food poisoning and it made me throw up.

THROUGH

BEEN THROUGH THE MILL (USUALLY PAST TENSE)

to have tough experiences

[tener malas experiencias]

Tom has had a tough life; he's been through the mill.

GET* THROUGH TO

SEE* THROUGH

SLIP **THROUGH*** ONE'S FINGERS

THROUGH THE **GRAPEVINE***

THROUGH **THICK*** AND THIN

THUMB

RULE OF THUMB

practical or estimated measure

[manera práctica de hacer algo[

I had no working plans for building the wagon. However, I managed to build it by rule of thumb.

BE UNDER SOMEONE'S THUMB

to be under someone's control

[bajo el control de alguien]

I have Tim under my thumb because he is afraid that I'll cut off his allowance; so he does anything I ask.

THUMBS

ALL THUMBS

clumsy

[torpe]

Lulu made a mess of sewing that hem; she was all thumbs.

THUMBS DOWN

no, rejected

[rechazado]

He said thumbs down to my request for a raise.

THUMBS UP

yes, approved

[aprobado]

Marie said thumbs up for celebrating my birthday.

TWIDDLE ONE'S THUMBS

to waste time, to do nothing

[perder tiempo, no hacer nada]

*Look under the **key word*** for this idiom.

Jason never helps me. He twiddled his thumbs while I mopped the floor.

WIN **HANDS*** DOWN (THUMBS DOWN).

THUNDER
STEAL* SOMEONE'S THUNDER

TICK
MAKE* (ONE) TICK

TICKER
BUM* TICKER

TICKLED
TICKLED **PINK*** (SILLY)

TIDE
TIDE SOMEONE OVER
to help someone during a difficult period
[ayudar a alguien por una temporada difícil]
Sally tided me over with groceries until I got a job.

TIE
TIE THE **KNOT***

TIED
FIT* TO BE TIED
ONE'S **HANDS*** ARE TIED

TIGHT
SIT* TIGHT
TIGHT **SQUEEZE***

TIGHTEN
TIGHTEN ONE'S **BELT***

TILL
HAVE ONE'S **HAND*** IN THE TILL
TILL THE **COWS*** COME HOME

TIME
BIDE* ONE'S TIME
FOR THE TIME **BEING***
GIVE* SOMEONE A HARD TIME
IN THE **NICK*** OF TIME
KEEP **GOOD*** TIME
MAKE **GOOD*** TIME
SERVE* (DO) TIME
TAKE* ONE'S TIME

TAKE* (TIME) OFF

TIP
TIP SOMEONE OFF; TIP OFF SOMEONE
to give someone information not generally known
[avisar a alguien]
I'm glad Dolly tipped me off that the fire inspectors were coming to check on the fire extinguishers.

TIRED
DOG* TIRED
SICK* AND TIRED

TIT
TIT FOR **TAT***

TLC
TLC
tender, loving care
[amor con ternura]
The puppy got lots of TLC from Mary.

TOM
EVERY TOM, **DICK*** AND HARRY

TOGETHER
PULL* ONESELF TOGETHER
PUT OUR (YOUR, THEIR) **HEADS*** TOGETHER

TON
LIKE A **TON*** OF BRICKS

TONGUE
BITE* ONE'S TONGUE
FORKED* TONGUE
GIVE* SOMEONE A TONGUE LASHING
HOLD* ONE'S TONGUE
SLIP* OF THE TONGUE
TONGUE IN **CHEEK***

TOOTH
TOOTH AND **NAIL***
WITH A FINE-TOOTHED **COMB***

TOP
OFF THE TOP OF ONE'S **HEAD***
SLEEP* LIKE A TOP
TOP-NOTCH
superior

[superior]
>   *Her swimming form is top-notch. She will be accepted on the swimming team.*

_____

TOP SOMETHING OR SOMEONE
to do better than someone or something
[superar algo o a alguien]
>   *Mimi topped the boys easily in 50 yard racing.*

_____

TOPSY-TURVY
TOPSY TURVY
upside down
[al revés]
>   *Everything in our house is topsy turvy because of the alterations and painting.*

_____

TOUCH
GET IN TOUCH WITH
to communicate with
[comunicarse con]
>   *I must get in touch with Mary; I haven't heard from her in a long time.*

_____

KEEP* IN TOUCH
LOSE* ONE'S TOUCH
PUT THE TOUCH (BITE*) ON SOMEONE
SOFT* TOUCH
TOUCH AND GO
uncertain
[dudoso]
>   *Tony's chances of surviving the car accident were touch and go.*

_____

TOUGH
TOUGH (HARD) NUT TO CRACK*

TOURIST
TOURIST TRAP

an establishment or area that attracts tourists, is overpriced, and often sells shoddy merchandise
[un lugar que atrae a los turistas, cobra mucho dinero, y a menudo vende mercancias de calidad baja]
>   *I warned Maria to beware of the tourist traps near the center of town, and to buy her souvenirs at reputable shops.*

_____

TOWEL
THROW IN THE TOWEL (SPONGE*)

TOWN
GO* TO TOWN
ONE-HORSE* TOWN
PAINT* THE TOWN RED

TRACK
ONE-TRACK MIND*
KEEP TRACK OF SOMEONE OR SOMETHING
to follow the activities of, or to keep records of
[mantenerse enterado de las actividades de]
>   *I found it hard to keep track of Lenny because he was involved in so many things and went from one place to another so quickly.*

_____

LOSE* TRACK OF SOMEONE
TRACK DOWN
to seek and find
[buscar y hallar]
>   *We needed the help of the Missing Persons Bureau to help track down Nicholas when he did not come home all week.*

_____

TRACKS
WRONG SIDE OF THE TRACKS
the section of town where the poorer people live
[el sector de la ciudad en donde vive la gente pobre]
>   *The bank president could not figure out how George, who came from the wrong side of the tracks, became so successful in the business world.*

_____

*Look under the **key word** for this idiom.

TRADE

A TRADE-IN

a used object given as partial payment for a purchase

[la cosa trocada]

The dealer offered me a $600 trade-in for my old car if I buy any car on display today.

TO TRADE IN SOMETHING; TO TRADE SOMETHING IN

to give a used item as partial payment for a purchase

[ofrecer alguna cosa de ocasión como parte del pago por una compra]

I traded my old car in when I bought my new car.

TRADES

JACK*-OF-ALL-TRADES

TRAIN

ON THE GRAVY* TRAIN

TRAP

TOURIST* TRAP

TREAT

DUTCH* TREAT

TRICK OR TREAT! (NO VARIATION!)

an expression used by children ringing neighbors' doorbells at Halloween time, threatening to play a harmful trick unless they are given a treat.

[una expresión usada por los niños cuando tocan el timbre de los vecinos en la víspera del Día de Todos los Santos, amen azando que van a hacer bromas dañosas si no reciben un regalo.]

Trick or treat! Trick or treat! Give me a present or I will drop an egg on your porch!

TREE

BARK* UP THE WRONG TREE

TRICK

DO THE TRICK

to be enough to accomplish a specific purpose

[ser suficiente para que algo se realice]

A Phillips screwdriver will do the trick in repairing the telephone.

MISS* A TRICK

TRICK OR TREAT*

TRICKS

PLAY TRICKS ON SOMEONE

to deceive someone

[decepciónar a alguien]

My eyes have been playing tricks on me lately. Sometimes I see double.

TRY

TRY ON SOMETHING

to wear something to see whether it is suitable in size, comfort, and appearance

[probar (una prenda de vestir)]

I tried on Harry's new suit, and it fit me perfect-

ly.

TRY SOMETHING OUT; TRY OUT SOMETHING

to use something to see whether it is satisfactory

[utilizar algo para ver si es apropiado]

I tried out the car on a test drive before

I decided to buy it.

TUBE

BOOB* TUBE

TUBES

DOWN THE TUBES (DRAIN*)

TUNE

WHISTLE A DIFFERENT* TUNE

TURKEY

COLD* TURKEY

TALK* TURKEY

TURN

TURN AROUND SOMETHING; TURN SOMETHING AROUND

to reverse

[volverse]

The police have turned around on the question of gun control. Recent killings of policemen by cheap handguns have forced the police to favor gun control.

TURN DOWN SOMEONE OR SOMETHING; TURN SOMEONE OR SOMETHING DOWN

to reject or to be rejected

[rechazar a]

Scott was disappointed when he was turned down for the role of Hamlet in the school play. .

TURN IN SOMEONE OR SOMETHING; TURN SOMEONE OR SOMETHING IN

(1) to report or deliver a wrongdoer to an authority

[denunciar o entregar a alguien que ha hecho una injuria]

Glenn turned in the three students who had cheated on the examination.

---

(2) to go to bed

[acostarse]

I am tired and sleepy. I am going to turn in for the night.

TURN SOMEONE OFF; TURN OFF SOMEONE

to repel someone

[repugnar a alguien]

Rudi is such a bore. He turns me off from the moment he starts talking.

TURN SOMEONE ON; TURN ON SOMEONE

to delight someone

[encantar a alguien]

The sound of country music turns me on.

TURN OUT

to end up

[resultar]

I know that the quilt you're working on will turn out beautifully.

TURN OUT

the number of people who attend

[el público (en un espectáculo)]

The turnout at the football game was very disappointing.

TURN OVER

(1) for a motor to start

[capotar]

My automobile engine stalled, and I could not get it to turn over.

---

(2) to turn to one's other side

[volcar]

I have a sharp pain in my left side whenever I turn over in bed.

TURN OVER A NEW **LEAF***
TURN SOMEONE'S **STOMACH***
TURN THE **TABLES*** ON
TURN **UPSIDE*** DOWN

TURNS
TAKE* TURNS

TURVY
TOPSY*-TURVY

TWENTY-TWO, 22
CATCH* 22

TWIDDLE
TWIDDLE ONE'S **THUMBS***

*Look under the **key word*** for this idiom.

TWIST
TWIST SOMEONE'S **ARM***
TWIST SOMEONE AROUND ONE'S **FINGER***

TWO
FEEL LIKE TWO **CENTS***
HAVE TWO **STRIKES*** AGAINST ONE
KILL TWO **BIRDS*** WITH ONE STONE
PUT IN ONE'S TWO **CENTS'*** WORTH
PUT* TWO AND TWO TOGETHER
STAND ON ONE'S OWN TWO **FEET***
TELL* SOMEONE A THING OR TWO
TWO-**FACED***

UNCLE
SAY (**CRY***) UNCLE

UNDER
GET* OUT FROM UNDER
GO* UNDER THE KNIFE
RIGHT UNDER ONE'S **NOSE***
UNDER SOMEONE'S **THUMB***
UNDER THE **TABLE***
UNDER THE **WEATHER***

UP
BE* UP TO
BUTTER* UP
CATCH* UP
CATCH UP TO SOMEONE
  to overtake
  [alcanzar a alguien]
    *Jennie has almost finished sewing her dress.
    Do you think you can catch up to her?*

CHALK* UP
CLAM* UP
COUGH* UP
COVER* UP
DOCTOR* UP
DOLL* UP
DRESS* UP
HANG* UP
HELD* UP
HOLD UP
   SEE **HELD UP***
KEEP ONE'S CHIN* UP
LET* UP
ON* THE UP AND UP

TO BE UP TO SOMETHING
to be doing something that others are not aware of
[hacer algo que los demás ignoran]
  *Vinnie has been acting peculiarly these past
  few days. I wonder what he is up to.*

UP A **CREEK*** (UP THE CREEK)
UP IN **ARMS***
UP AGAINST THE **WALL***
UP AND ABOUT
  active
  [activo]
    *Mom was up and about two weeks after her
    appendectomy.*

UP **FRONT***
UP TO SOMEONE
  someone's choice or responsibility
  [la responsabilidad de alguien]
    Whether you go on this trip is completely up to you.

UP THE **RIVER***
UP TO **DATE***
UP TO ONE'S **EARS***
UP TO **PAR***
WAIT* UP
WASHED* UP
WHOOP* IT UP

UPPER
GET* THE UPPER HAND
KEEP A STIFF UPPER **LIP***

UPSET
UPSET THE APPLE **CART***

UPSIDE
TURN SOMETHING UPSIDE DOWN
  to disorganize, to mess things up
  [desorganizar]
    *I've turned this room upside down looking for
    my tennis shoes.*

USE
USE ONE'S NOODLE (HEAD*)

USED
BE USED TO
to be accustomed to
[estar acostumbrado a]
> *I am used to having Mattie drop in for tea every afternoon on his way home from work.*

VAIN
BE IN VAIN
to be useless
[en balde]
> *I spent hours trying to repair the doghouse, but it was all in vain.*

VAMOOSE
VAMOOSE! (No variation!)
Go away!
[¡Vete! ¡Váya(n)se!]
> *Please don't hang around in front of this store any longer. Vamoose!*

VOICE
HAVE A VOICE IN
to vote or influence an outcome
[votar o influir en un asunto]
> *Parents should have a voice in setting the school calendar, the dates when schools are open and closed.*

WAD
SHOOT* ONE'S WAD

WAGON
FIX* ONE'S WAGON

ON THE WAGON
abstaining from liquor
[renunciando al acohol]
> *I've been on the wagon for three months and I'm feeling great.*

WAIT
WAIT ON SOMEONE
to serve
[servir]
> *Florence waited on us at The Blue Grill Cafe, and she served us very well.*

WAIT UP FOR SOMEONE
to remain awake while waiting for
[velar en espera de]
> *Mr. Jones waited up for his daughter to come home from the prom.*

WALK
WALK ALL OVER SOMEONE
to treat someone badly
[maltratar a alguien]
> *Our new supervisor tried to walk all over me, but she stopped when she found that I would not tolerate such treatment.*

*Look under the **key word*** for this idiom.

WALKING

GIVE* SOMEONE WALKING PAPERS

WALL

DRIVE SOMEONE UP A WALL

to make someone angry

[sacarle a alguien de quicio]

Lulu drives me up a wall when she tells that old story about how she became a success.

_____

HAVE ONE'S **BACK*** TO THE WALL

KNOCK* ONE'S HEAD AGAINST THE WALL

TALK* TO THE WALL

BE UP AGAINST THE WALL

to have almost no choices

[desperado]

After six months without a job, and no savings, Abner started selling apples because he was up against the wall.

_____

WARPATH

BE ON THE WARPATH

to be angry and prepared to fight

[enojado y listo a pelear]

I stay away from Lou. He has been on the warpath lately, and I don't know exactly what he expects.

_____

WART

WORRYWART

someone who constantly worries about everything

[persona que se preocupa constantemente]

Lee is a terrible worrywart. She can think up new worries more quickly than anyone else I know.

_____

WASH

WASH ONE'S **HANDS*** OF

WASHED

BE WASHED UP

to be unsuccessful

[fracasado]

Ruth is all washed up as a dressmaker in this shop, since she did such a bad job sewing those party dresses.

_____

WASTE

WASTE ONE'S **BREATH***

WATCH

WATCH OUT FOR SOMEONE OR SOMETHING

(1) to look carefully for

[buscar]

Watch out for Jennie. Let me know when she comes out of school, because I promised to take her home.

_____

(2) to beware of

[tener cuidado con]

Watch out for splinters on that wooden floor.

_____

WATCHER

CLOCK*-WATCHER

WATER

COME* HELL OR HIGH WATER

BE IN HOT WATER

to be in trouble

[en líos]

Kelly is in hot water. He was arrested for stealing, and this is his third offense..

_____

KEEP ONE'S **HEAD*** ABOVE WATER

LIKE A **FISH*** OUT OF WATER

MAKE* SOMEONE'S MOUTH WATER

THROW **COLD*** WATER ON

WATER DOWN SOMETHING; WATER SOMETHING DOWN

to dilute

[diluir]

The science course was watered down so that everyone could pass it. .

_____

WAVELENGTH

BE ON THE SAME WAVELENGTH

to have the same attitude, interest or opinion

[estar de acuerdo]

Manny and I are good friends because we are usually on the same wavelength.

WAVES

MAKE* WAVES

WAY

GET* ONE'S OWN WAY (HAVE ONE'S WAY)

to do what one wants

[hacer lo que se le antoje a uno]

I usually let Gary have his own way, unless what he wants to do is dangerous for him or someone else.

IN THE WORST WAY

very much

[muchísimo]

I want that leather jacket in the worst way.

MAKE* ONE'S OWN WAY

NO WAY! (No variation!)

Absolutely not!

[¡De ninguna manera!]

Mr. Green said "No way!" to Paul's request to drive his car Saturday night.

RUB* SOMEONE THE WRONG WAY

TO BE IN SOMEONE'S WAY

to obstruct someone

[estorbar a alguien]

Paul is in my way to getting a promotion on the job.

WEAR

WEAR DOWN SOMETHING; WEAR SOMETHING DOWN.

to reduce the size of something by using it

[desgastar algo]

I used those sandals so much that I quickly wore down the heels and soles.

WEAR DOWN SOMEONE

to make someone so weary they can't say "No."

[cansar]

She wore me down with her nagging for sweets so that I finally let her have another ice cream cone.

WEAR OFF

to diminish

[disminuir]

Keep Pat in bed until the effects of his upset stomach wear off.

WEAR OUT SOMETHING; WEAR SOMETHING OUT

(1) to make useless because of overuse

[hacer inútil por mucho uso]

Shoes are a big expense in this family because John wears his out so quickly.

(2) to exhaust

[rendir]

After a day of cooking, cleaning and taking care of the children, Mom is worn out.

WEAR THE PANTS*

WEASEL

WEASEL OUT OF (GET OUT OF)

to avoid in a sneaky way

[evitar con maa]

Jim tried to weasel out of painting the fence by complaining about a sudden allergy to the smell of paint.

_____

WEATHER
BE UNDER THE WEATHER
to be sick
[enfermo]
> *Sally won't be coming to visit this afternoon. She is a bit under the weather.*

_____

WEIGHT
PUT* ON WEIGHT
THROW* ONE'S WEIGHT AROUND

WELL
WELL-HEELED
wealthy
[adinerado]
> *Jack is well-heeled; he inherited a lot of money from an uncle.*

_____

WELL OFF
(1) comfortable financially
[en un buen estado financiero]
> *If I stay with this company and get promotions regularly, I should be well off in ten years and not have to worry about money.*

_____

(2) in a good situation
[de buenas condiciones]
> *My wardrobe is good, I have nice things to wear, and I am pretty well off in terms of clothing.*

_____

WET
ALL WET
all wrong
[completamente incorrecto]

Pay no attention to Sid's directions. He's all wet. Use a road map.

_____

GET ONE'S **FEET*** WET
WET **BEHIND*** THE EARS
WET **BLANKET***

WHEELER
WHEELER-**DEALER***

WHEELS
SPIN* ONE'S WHEELS

WHERE
LET THE **CHIPS*** FALL WHERE THEY MAY

WHISTLE
BLOW* THE WHISTLE
WHISTLE A **DIFFERENT*** TUNE

WHITE
WHITE **ELEPHANT***

WHO'S
WHO'S WHO
a list of persons who have achieved fame by their accomplishments
[un libro que contiene una lista de personas que han logrado la fama por sus actividades]
> *Two of Mrs. Green's sons are listed in WHO'S WHO. She is very proud of them.*

_____

WHOLE
ON THE WHOLE
in general
[por lo general]
> *Our school has some bad points, but on the whole it is pretty good.*

_____

WHOOP
WHOOP IT UP
to celebrate in a noisy, boisterous way
[celebrar con ruido]

After the prom, we whooped it up outside the school.

_____

WILD
A WILD GOOSE **CHASE***

WIN
WIN **HANDS*** DOWN

WIND
GET* WIND OF

WIND (WRAP) UP
to end, to finish
[terminarse, terminar]
The party wound up at midnight. Everyone went home. After four hours, we wrapped up the deal.

_____

WING
WING IT
to do something without preparation, but relying instead on one's general knowledge and experience
[improvisar]
The substitute teacher had to wing it when she covered the Science class without notice.

_____

WINKS
FORTY* WINKS

WIPED
TO BE WIPED OUT
(1) to tire
[estar cansadísimo]
When the housepainters finished painting the apartment, I was completely wiped out.

_____

(2) to lose all one's money
[perder uno todo su dinero]
Our old neighbor, Mr. Faulkner told us how, in 1929, when the stock market crashed, he was wiped out.

_____

(3) to be exterminated
[estar exterminado]
The dolphins and the tuna have almost been wiped out because of excessive fishing.

_____

WIRE
JUST UNDER THE WIRE
at the last moment
[al ultimo momento]
We arrived at the theatre just under the wire. The curtain was going up.

_____

LIVE* WIRE

WISECRACK
WISECRACK
a comment that is meant to be funny
[una salida sarcástica]
Phil makes many wisecracks, but they are not usually as funny as he thinks they are.

_____

WISHY-WASHY
WISHY-WASHY
without a definite opinion
[indeciso]
Deb is never wishy-washy. She always knows exactly what she wants to do.

_____

WIT'S
AT ONE'S WIT'S **END***

WOLF
CRY* WOLF
KEEP THE WOLF FROM THE **DOOR***
WOLF IN SHEEP'S **CLOTHING***

WONDER
NO WONDER
not surprising; reasonable
[¡Con razón!]

*Look under the **key word*** for this idiom.

No wonder you can't get that stain out of your coat. You've been using the wrong soap.

Jim works out every morning for one hour; he finds it invigorating.

WOODS
BE OUT OF THE WOODS
to be safe; to have found a solution
[en salvo]
> *I have finally solved this computer problem that has been giving me so much trouble. I'm not out of the woods yet but it won't take me long to finish the job.*

WOOL
PULL THE WOOL OVER SOMEONE'S **EYES***

WORD
BREATHE* A WORD
MUM'S* THE WORD
TAKE ONE AT ONE'S WORD
to believe someone
[creer a alguien]
> *He says that he will repay you tomorrow. Please take him at his word.*

WORD OF **MOUTH***

WORDS
EAT* ONE'S WORDS
TAKE THE WORDS OUT OF SOMEONE'S **MOUTH***

WORK
WORK AROUND THE **CLOCK***
WORK OUT
(1) to solve a problem
[resolver un problema]
> *I worked out the solution to the geometry problem very easily.*

(2) to exercise
[hacer ejercicios]

WORLD
OUT OF THIS WORLD
wonderful, marvelous
[maravilloso]
> *The fall colors in the Northeast are out of this world. The trees look like an artist's palette.*

WORSE
HIS **BARK*** IS WORSE THAN HIS BITE

WORST
IN THE WORST **WAY***

WORTH
PUT IN ONE'S TWO **CENTS'*** WORTH

WRAP
WIND* (WRAP) UP

WRINGER
PUT* THROUGH THE WRINGER

WRONG
BARK* UP THE WRONG TREE
GET OFF ON THE WRONG **FOOT***
GET UP ON THE WRONG SIDE OF THE **BED***
RUB* SOMEONE THE WRONG WAY
START OFF ON THE WRONG **FOOT***
WRONG SIDE OF THE **TRACKS***

YELL
YELL (SCREAM) **BLOODY*** MURDER

YOKEL
LOCAL* YOKEL

YOU
YOU KNOW
a phrase used by many people that means nothing but gives the speaker time to select his next words
[Es una expresión que mucha gente usa en una pausa en su discurso, entre palabras. (En español se usa "este" de una manera parecida.]

As I was saying, you know, the teacher asked me to stand up, you know, and then told me that my composition was pretty good, you know.

YOU'RE
YOU'RE **KIDDING!***

Z
FROM **A*** TO Z

ZIP
ZIP ONE'S **LIP***

*Look under the **key word*** for this idiom.

Notes

Notes

Notes

Notes

Notes